CONFRONTATIONAL POLITICS

CONFRONTATIONAL POLITICS

Senator H. L. Richardson (ret.)

Titles from Jameson Books are available at special discounts for bulk purchases, for sales promotions, premiums, fund raising or educational use. Special condensed or excerpted paperback editions can also be created to customer specifications.

For information and other requests please write Jameson Books, Inc., 722 Columbus Street, P.O. Box 738, Ottawa, Illinois 61350.

Mail Orders: 800-426-1357
Telphone: 815-434-7905
Facsimile: 815-434-7907
Email: jamesonbooks@yahoo.com

Printed in the United States of America.

Jameson Books are distributed to the book trade by MidPoint Trade Books, 27 West 20th Street, Suite 1102, New York, NY 10011. Bookstores please call 212-727-0190 to place orders.

Bookstore returns should be addressed to MidPoint Trade Books, 1263 Southwest Boulevard, Kansas City, KS 66103.

ISBN: 978-0-915463-76-3

5 4 3 2 1 12 11 10 09

Contents

Foreword

Some conservatives still linger under the misapprehension that being right, in the sense of being correct, is sufficient to win in the public policy process. If you can prove you're right, they believe, victory will fall into your hands like a ripe fruit off of a tree.

That's not true, of course. Victory in political battles in the long run is determined by the number and the effectiveness of the activists on the respective sides.

Potential activists, in large numbers, can be identified, recruited, trained, and led to victories, provided that leaders teach them that they owe it to their philosophy to study how to win.

Conservatives who have learned this lesson have made "conservative" the most popular label of choice in American politics and won many, many battles for their principles.

This did not happen by accident. There were pioneers who figured out the *real* nature of politics, practiced what they discovered, and taught others.

Former State Senator H. L. "Bill" Richardson of California is one of the most important of those pioneers, and he's still a major conservative force in politics.

Many years ago, Bill Richardson's little book, *Slightly to the Right*, reached me at the right time in my life. That gem is now available free online (see page 111).

I had been Barry Goldwater's youngest elected delegate to the 1964 Republican National Convention, and I wanted to devote myself to advancing conservative principles. *Slightly to the Right* had a great impact on me.

Bill Richardson's writings combine a clear-cut commitment to conservative philosophy, a wicked sense of humor, and an almost unique understanding of practical politics. In sum, for many conservative activists and leaders he's been an inspiration.

This new and revised edition of his most popular book, *Confrontational Politics*, also comes at an appropriate time.

Conservatives have had to cope with some problems of success.

Before 1980 our very survival was in question. Everyone who called himself a conservative did so despite the perception that we were on the losing side. Unity is easier for an embattled minority.

Today, many opportunists and content-free Republicans adopt the conservative label as protective coloration, and the conservative coalition itself seems divided into half a dozen squabbling factions. Many of these divisions will fade in importance during the period of Democrat hegemony which began with the 2008 elections.

Meanwhile, the left seems more united than ever. They have drummed conservatives out of the Democratic Party. The major news media continue to root for leftist political candidates, for leftist legislation, and for leftist judges. And academia consists mainly of leftist indoctrination centers.

But conservatives should not worry too much about our unity in future battles with the left, even though there are some among us who will say, "It's not enough for you to agree with my position on almost every issue. If you're not for it for all the same reasons, to hell with you!"

In general elections and big legislative battles, we all usually have only two candidates to choose from, or the choice of supporting or opposing a bill. When push comes to shove, almost all leading proponents of limited government, free enterprise, strong national defense, and traditional moral values tend to unite.

The two things that count are the number and the effectiveness of the leaders and activists on the respective sides.

It's not enough merely to oppose the left; we must study how to oppose them so effectively that we win.

Bill Richardson, by his example and through his writing, has a *lot* to teach conservatives who want to win.

In *Framed*, a book bemoaning the success of conservatives in throwing out liberal judges in California, leftist author Betty Medsger states:

> Richardson has found a way to turn Reagan's anti-judiciary attacks into more than rhetoric. Richardson doesn't just lament liberal judges, he has created the means of removing them.... Richardson single-handedly changed the unwritten rules.... He's a California combination of Jesse Helms and Richard Viguerie.... He's a politician with a flair for his original occupation, advertising and public relations.... Richardson's politics put him slightly to the right of Attila the Hun, an assertion he would probably take as a compliment. But he can be as charming as Fred Astaire.... Numerous legislators have been defeated not by any grass-roots organization in their own district but by Richardson coming into their district and financing an opponent handpicked by him.... This California story is important for the country.

Bill Richardson served as a California state senator for 22 years (1966–88).

In 1975, he was a member of the national executive committee of the National Rifle Association (NRA). In those days, NRA's idea of political action was to send, say, $500 to an incumbent legislator.

Bill convinced NRA's leadership of the need for more political action and more pro-Second Amendment organizations. With Richard Viguerie doing his direct mail, Bill created two political action committees (PACs): Gun Owners of California and Gun Owners of America. He still heads both groups.

These two PACs were an immediate success with the gun community and worked to elect more pro-gunners and defeat more gun grabbers. He kept his groups' administrative size small and spent big bucks in campaigns.

To process his new groups' voluminous mail, he created Computer Caging Corporation. That grew into an excellent direct mail business that helped conservative candidates.

Bill recruited Sgt. John Feliz, then with the Los Angeles Police Force, to run a new political action committee, the Law and Order Campaign Committee (LOCC).

A relatively unknown state senator named George Deukmejian had run last in a previous race for attorney general, without the support of Bill Richardson.

Next time, things went differently.

Deukmejian introduced a death penalty bill, which Richardson had co-authored. The Democrats held majorities in both houses of the state legislature.

Governor Jerry Brown had said he would veto a death penalty bill if it reached his desk. Sen. Richardson and LOCC stirred up public support for the bill, which narrowly passed. Governor Moonbeam vetoed it, as promised.

Making a statewide hero of Sen. George Deukmejian (the bill's major author), Sen. Richardson and LOCC generated so much pressure through the mails that the legislature overrode the veto by two-thirds votes in both houses.

The next time Deukmejian ran for attorney general, he won. Then he ran for governor and won. His defeated opponent, Los Angeles Mayor Tom Bradley, attributed his loss to Proposition 15, the gun issue he had supported—another victory for the strategy and tactics of Bill Richardson.

In 1978, LOCC took a leadership role in asking for a "no" vote in the statewide election on the confirmation of the far-left Rose Bird, the California Supreme Court's Chief Justice. Such an effort was unprecedented. People thought Bill Richardson and his people were crazy to try it, but Rose Bird barely survived the vote.

Undaunted, Bill and his groups kept up the fight against Bird. They enjoyed every minute of the effort. Eight years later, the voters not only threw out Chief Justice Rose Bird by over a million votes but also removed two of her liberal fellow justices.

Bill also set up FREEPAC, a small-to-medium-sized business PAC, and raised over $100,000 to put into campaigns. It had great promise.

However, the opposition finally got smart and passed legislation prohibiting legislators from having more than two PACs. Since only one legislator, Bill Richardson, had more than two, guess who they had in mind?

Bill voluntarily left the legislature in 1988 and keeps himself busy writing, consulting, overseeing the two gun organizations, and being a good Christian husband and grandfather.

You can bet he takes personal satisfaction these days watching so many liberals dive for cover on the gun issue. They realize it's no longer a winning cause for them.

In *Confrontational Politics*, Bill Richardson shares an enormous number of lessons he has learned, some of them learned the hard way, in his long and successful political career.

This book is fun to read, and conservatives who study it carefully and follow Bill's advice systematically will win a lot more battles in the future.

Morton C. Blackwell
Virginia Republican
National Committeeman

Introduction

Confrontation has the potential to be unpleasant and upsetting. Angry confrontation conjures up "in your face" situations which most people deplore. When applied to the political arena, it is doubly onerous. "Smash mouth" politics comes to mind, a situation that turns people off.

Those of us who espouse traditional American values must understand that contemporary confrontational politics isn't of our making. It is, however, the foundation of the tactics successfully practiced by the leaders of the radical left. We must understand their methodology in order to combat them effectively. Combat them we must. To do otherwise would be to abdicate the field of American politics which is, upon reflection, unthinkable, not to mention moral cowardice.

As this is written, the liberal left dominates the Democratic Party and is trying to penetrate the Republican Party as well. Hence, to effectively combat the left, we must know how to stand up to them, which means learning the art of *effective* confrontation.

Occasionally, well-meaning souls confuse the harmful (indeed, I believe, evil) ends of the left with their methods and tactics, some of which are also evil (like lying) and some of which are morally neutral (like confrontation). These nice folks then object to confrontation saying, "The ends do not justify the means." However, it is the left's ends that are, in fact, evil.

I

Confronting evil is a positive act. Instead of just fighting a defensive battle, we must understand how to take advantage of the left's many weaknesses and leverage their mistakes to our advantage.

But how do we do this? After a lifetime devoted to active participation in American political affairs I can confidently affirm that knowledgeable use of our values combined with practical knowledge of leftist tactics is the most effective way to defeat the enemies of traditional American values.

Opinion is not power; accurate knowledge is. The humorist Will Rogers stated it best, "Ignorance ain't our problem, it's all that we know that ain't true."

President Theodore Roosevelt said, "I believe the next half century will determine if we will advance the cause of Christian civilization or revert to the horrors of brutal paganism."

How right he was. Anyone who doesn't believe paganism is alive and thriving, doesn't understand paganism or hasn't turned on a TV in the last several decades and watched the battle taking place between the ideas of the pagans and the patriarchs. That's what this political opus is about—the nature of the battle of ideas.

Book introductions are usually boring—this one is no exception. But stick with me because there are some concepts in the next paragraphs worth thinking about and maybe even worth remembering.

A wise American by the name of Richard Weaver once remarked, "Ideas have consequences." How very true; these three words have huge significance when they are backed by actions. Some ideas can have great impact, giving birth to nations, starting wars—changing history.

America is now suffering from a conflict flowing from two diametrically opposed beliefs. It is a deadly war of immense consequence, affecting the moral fiber of our country. The two combatants are radical humanists and those of us who adhere to traditional American values—what I called above "the pagans and the patriarchs." Paradoxically, both stem from opposite sides of the same coin. *The fundamental concept that undergirds each belief system is its view of God. One believes He exists and is relevant, and the other that He does not exist or that He does not really matter.*

Let's look at what behavior flows from each side of these contrary ideas.

It is a fact that, consciously or unconsciously, adherence to a given ideology usually results in predictable behavior. How each of us is intellectually trained has a direct impact on how we act or more often react; often with predictable consequences. Basic assumptions are the railroad tracks where the train of thought invariably goes.

Morals and methodology, ideas and subsequent action, are intrinsically intertwined. So, what happens politically when one raised with traditional American values comes in contact with a fellow American adhering to contemporary humanist dogma? In politics, it is obvious that confrontation is the inevitable result— often desired and manipulated by the radical liberals and disliked and misunderstood by traditional Americans.

This to me is a word painting about the "abstract art" of political confrontation, the unpleasant scene that inevitably occurs when divergent beliefs come into contact with each other. I use the word "art" because the study of politics is not a science, despite what academics and political consultants are prone to claim, and the adjective "abstract" because politics isn't easily understood.

The wild colors of politics deal with two of the most complicated and explosive paints on earth—power and people.

However abstract, the study of the political methodology of both liberals and traditional Americans is a worthy venture. Serious investigation into this subject yields a surprising amount of certainty and profit. To achieve this requires investigation into the fundamentals that underscore the traditionalists and our antithesis—the radical humanists.

Before we can solve any problem we must understand its component parts. "A problem well stated is a problem half solved," said American inventor Charles F. Kettering. Knowledge of the subject matter usually defines and dictates the solution. This is true in politics as well as in any other discipline. In this case, we should know how the opposition thinks and the methods that flow from their basic beliefs.

We must also understand ourselves. When one consistently loses political ground, it is imperative to ask honest, introspective questions about why losses occur.

I contend our ideas are valid and ultimately defensible. Therefore, if it's not our ideas, then it is the conservative American methodology and tactics of combating the left that is our problem.

In fact, the average conservative has little knowledge regarding the techniques he unconsciously uses in political battle. Indeed, the conservative frequently refuses to admit he or she is even in a political battle.

The central battle theme of this book centers on the methods employed in this vital conflict. The purpose is to inspect both combatants and the methods each uses.

By now, conservatives should recognize that being "right" isn't enough; if that's all it took, we would have won long ago.

Two thousand five hundred years ago Sun Tsu, the famous Chinese general and sage, wrote in his book *The Art of War,* "Know thy enemy as well as thyself." Notice, Sun Tsu said "know thyself" as well as knowing the enemy. Self-inspection hasn't been a conservative strong suit. Instead of looking inward, a great number of conservatives have found solace in blaming either our opponent, the referee, or the audience. This is a bad habit too many have sadly acquired. (We should remember an old saying, "A fox always sniffs his own den first.")

1

Why Traditional American Habits Prevent Conservatives from Successfully Countering the Left

A number of years ago I was teaching some fellow conservatives the methodology needed to effectively debate our fuzzy friends and liberal acquaintances. At the conclusion of the class, I asked two of the students to debate a given issue. One was to take the liberal side and the other the conservative. The man selected to argue the conservative position was an extremely bright, articulate young lawyer by the name of Lou (a graduate of Yale and chief administrative assistant to a popular conservative congressman). The conservative, Gary, whom I asked to play the liberal, was also extremely capable, a Stanford graduate with a master's degree in English.

Within a minute, Lou was in trouble and, before long, found himself on the defensive, being chewed up by Gary, the conservative arguing the liberal line. I stopped the debate and asked the lawyer why he wasn't using the techniques he had just recently been taught. His response was very informative. He answered, "I don't like to argue that way."

What the young lawyer was really saying was that his conservative Christian upbringing had formed patterns of response that dictated his behavior and, even though he now knew better, he felt guilty answering any other way.

Sound confusing? Not if you understand someone who's been raised with traditional American values. Lou, like most conservatives, had been raised to be direct in response to questions. To be evasive—not to answer forthrightly—is considered to be somewhat deceitful. Lou, like many of us, had been taught from childhood to look people in the eye and be brief, direct, and honest. He, as a child, had been admonished to be polite, considerate, and respectful of the opinions of others. Any other response is considered pushy, brash, and confrontational. So when Gary, playing the liberal position, changed the subject by asking a question, Lou, politely went along and directly answered. And at that point, Lou was trapped on the defensive, responding to Gary's statements and accusations.

Lou, like most Americans, believes in clearly defined right and wrong. In discussions, he prefers to come to conclusions, make statements, and end sentences with periods and exclamation marks. Not so the liberal.

Liberals have no moral compulsion to be direct or to answer any question asked of them. If they don't like the subject they will subtly change the direction of the conversation by asking a question. Their sentences end in question marks. They will quickly change the topic and ask a question in order to put the conservative on the defensive. The conservative, polite by nature, rarely attempts to keep the liberal on the subject by insisting that he stay on the original matter being discussed. Instead, the conservative bites— and true to form—tries to answer the new question asked by the liberal, thereby finding himself far afield from where he originally started.

Lou, the young lawyer, had been taught in my class to keep the liberal on the subject. But, his conservative self-image, his methodology of answering straightforwardly and directly, wouldn't let him. He was a victim of his own methodology, a way of responding that really had nothing to do with right and wrong. He could have smiled pleasantly, then quietly and firmly insisted that Gary stay on the subject.

An important fact to be learned is that knowledge is not necessarily behavior. One can "know" something but not necessarily live it or practice it. We "know" we shouldn't overeat, but we often do. We "know" we shouldn't drive too fast or drive after having a drink, but many do it anyway. In many instances, knowledge doesn't translate into overcoming ingrained habits.

6

It takes practice to overcome the desire to not answer a liberal's verbal change of direction, just as it takes determination to keep him on the subject.

The examples are legion. The conservative brings up the governmental fiscal irresponsibility in the welfare system and the liberal quickly changes the subject by asking, "Have you no regard for the poor? What do you want to do, get rid of welfare and let them starve?"

Or the conservative points out the inequality in so-called affirmative action programs and immediately he is asked a question that categorizes him as a bigot.

Or the conservative believes in the citizen's right to own semi-automatic firearms and the liberal's immediate response is to paint the conservative as one who supports ownership of *fully* automatic assault machine guns and the killing of children in school yards.

The list goes on and on. Argue for a strong national defense and they accuse you of wanting a nuclear war or to slaughter innocent women and children. Investigate foreign subversives and they twist it into McCarthyism. The list is endless.

In each case, the liberal changes the subject and the conservative, not wanting to be considered rude, goes along and inevitably answers the new question with a statement, soon finding himself sputtering and defending an untenable position.

And once a liberal gets an opponent into a defensive position, he pounds the conservative into dust.

Why does this happen? Why does the conservative allow this to occur? To understand this phenomenon, one needs to study Christian ethics and the methodology that flows from it. It is extremely difficult to understand present day America without knowledge of past "ideas" and the training that influences our present behavior.

For centuries, the vast preponderance of Americans believed in the Almighty as revealed in Scripture, the Bible—God, who mandates specific action and invokes judgment upon those who disobey. The belief in an all-powerful, all-knowing Deity had a distinct and definite behavioral impact upon the citizenry and, consequently, on how our remarkable society was formed. Such a God serves as governor of all conduct, looking constantly over each shoulder and into each heart. God's law is the basis for one's conscience, the framework for one's innermost thoughts and the behavior that flows from them.

As an example of how this viewpoint impacts behavior, notice how lying to anyone involves a very important third party—the Almighty—one who logs it all down for future judgment. Scripture is abundantly clear about what constitutes evil. Cheating, stealing, murdering, coveting the property of others, lasciviousness, homosexuality, and adultery; these acts are sinful and an abomination to the Lord, thus they are an abomination to the believer. Conversely, truthfulness, generosity, kindness, honesty, respect for the rights of others, the sanctity of life, fidelity, responsibility for children, honoring parents, civility, and protecting the property of others becomes desired and accepted behavior.

Such training begins in early childhood and is embedded in our marrow. As we grow up, our peers reinforce it. By the time we reach adulthood, it is ingrained into our personality and forms the basis for our conscience, thereby formulating our actions.

Most adults, upon reflection, recall having been admonished by parents: "Share with others," "Don't tell lies," "Respect the opinions of others since they are God's children, too," "Honesty is the best policy," "Do unto others as you would have them do unto you," "Don't be quick to judge," "Be thankful for what you have," "Nobody likes a braggart." The book of Proverbs served as the textbook for the conduct of our fathers as well as their fathers before them. In the 1800s, dried fruit was a staple because in winter months fresh produce wasn't available. It was a common saying that the citizenry was raised on "prunes and proverbs."

Due to this ethical training, the conservative perceives himself and others as singularly unique, individualistic, spiritual, worthy, and created in the image of his Maker. He is even instructed to love his enemies as well as his neighbors, and above all, to love and fear God.

At this point it is important to understand what constitutes "loving your enemies." It doesn't mean the emotional affection one feels for family and friends but rather, to treat all people by the standards of biblical law. In other words don't cheat, lie, steal, and covet, to/from anyone, not even your worst enemy. You wouldn't want it done to you, so don't do it to others. That doesn't mean you have to like them, hug them, or display affection for the opposition. However, it does mean we must always be civil.

Christian Puritan ethics were a dominant factor in all walks of American life for most of our nation's history. Political dissertations were filled with biblical quotations; the Bible was used as an authoritative and powerful document when proving a political point. No better example could be given than the comment of 81-year-old Benjamin Franklin, who at the Constitutional Convention stated the following to the assembled delegates. "I have lived, sirs, a long time, and the longer I live, the more convincing proofs I have seen of this truth—that God governs in the affairs of men. And if a sparrow cannot fall to the ground without His notice, is it probable that an empire can rise without His aid? We have been assured, sirs, in the Sacred Writings, that 'except the Lord build the house, they labor in vain that build it.'"

What could be a more convincing comment on the intent of the Founding Fathers than the statement of the respected Ben Franklin to the assembled delegates? Jonathan Dayton, a delegate from New Jersey, stated, "The words of the venerable Franklin fell upon our ears with a weight and authority, even greater than we may suppose an oracle to have had in a Roman Senate."

But by the beginning of the so-called "enlightened" twentieth century, the rumblings of humanism could be heard in America. President Theodore Roosevelt stated, "There are those who believe that a new modernity demands a new morality. What they fail to consider is the harsh reality that there is no such thing as a new morality. There is only one morality. All else is immorality. There is only true Christian ethics over against which stands the whole of paganism. If we are to fulfill our great destiny as a people, then we must return to the old morality, the sole morality."

President Roosevelt's scathing comments continued. "All these blatant sham reformers, in the name of a new morality, preach the old, old vice and self-indulgence which rotted out first the moral fiber and then even the external greatness of Greece and Rome."

Heavily influenced by their Judeo-Christian training, our ancestors recognized human capabilities, but also acknowledged our imperfections. Multi-faceted and capable as God's ultimate creation of man may be, he is not perfect nor is he perfectible in this world. Fallible and sinful, man is in continual need of God's grace and forgiveness for the perennial breaking of God's well-defined laws.

Having lived under the arbitrary power of the English parliament and under the foot of the imperial King George III, our forefathers realized the necessity to limit the power of man and government—in perpetuity. To do so, they drafted the United States Constitution, a document limiting governmental power, restricting and confining the powers of the central government. The public concern for liberty demanded even more guarantees of freedom, and the Bill of Rights was soon forthcoming.

The writers wisely did not want too much authority residing in the hands of fallible man, nor did they desire his errors to be codified into law.

Christianity teaches that all humans are precious in the eyes of God; each one is important, blessed with a soul, unique, capable of being one of God's children. As God's supreme creation, we have been given dominion over the earth—an awesome responsibility. Christians believe human life is infinitely more important than any other living thing. We are stewards, God's agents, held responsible for the proper care and management of everything therein. The guidebook, the management manual on how we should keep dominion, is the Holy Bible.

What then constitutes the behavior of a biblically influenced American citizen? Isn't he to be humble, respectful of another's opinion, even when he disagrees? Doesn't he usually keep his own counsel, responding only when asked, not rudely interrupting others, letting everyone "have his say"? When asked his opinion, should he not respond directly, punctually, honestly, expressing his true feelings?

What is expected when dealing with fellow citizens: disharmony, antagonism, disruptive hateful actions, and evasion? No—to the contrary. *Harmony is the desired social condition.*

Friendly, cooperative, respectful behavior is not only desired but also mandated by custom and culture. Even in business, "The customer is always right" policy reflects that view.

Argumentative, combative, demanding attitudes are frowned upon and avoided. The key word is HARMONY. When antagonism threatens, compromise is the accepted way to restore peaceful relationships. Giving of oneself, sacrificing in order to reach agreement, is deemed noble as long as no Commandment is broken. To be polite and considerate of others is the desired behavior. In dealing with those who accept and live by the same fundamental concepts, harmony is usually achieved; this is Christian action.

Controversy and confrontation are usually avoided for they make those who are consciously reared with Christian principles decidedly uncomfortable. Unconsciously, they may even experience guilt if they prolong or contribute to the controversy. Confrontation evokes negative emotions and is perceived as unsociable behavior leading to anger, even violence. Christianity breeds gentle people, gentlemen and ladies. To be called a gentleman is a compliment—even today.

To repeat, confrontation to the average American is an uncomfortable, unbecoming attitude to be avoided whenever possible. This methodology of avoidance is a habit deeply ingrained in traditional American patterns of behavior. This, combined with ignorance of humanist methodology, makes the average American very vulnerable, the victim of his own decency.

2

Humanism's Man-Centered Roots Necessarily Yield the Bitter Fruit of Political Domination and Oppression

Webster's dictionary of the 1970s defines humanism as follows: "A modern, non-theistic, rationalist movement that holds that man is capable of self-fulfillment and ethical conduct without recourse to supernaturalism. This intellectual and cultural secular movement stemmed from the study of classical literature and culture during the Middle Ages and was one of the factors giving rise to the Renaissance."

Sounds pretty fancy doesn't it? Intellectual, classical, cultural, giving rise to the Renaissance. From reading this definition, one could conclude that humanism's been around for a long time, a respected, age-old, philosophical movement of intellectuals. Not so. Humanism is another contemporary pagan version of ageless atheism, another attempt by man to build a new tower of Babel.

Webster's original dictionary of 1828 doesn't even have a definition for the word "humanism." If humanism had been around to give rise to the Renaissance, one would think Webster's dictionary of 1828 would have mentioned it. It didn't. Webster's did mention atheism.

Historically, man has chosen to reject God, thereby usurping for himself the exalted position. It's pretty hot stuff to think you can play God, but it's insanity to think you can get away with it. History is replete with man making a fool of himself, and modern man is no exception. There has always been a proliferation of cults offering multiple gods or lesser human deities to worship, each filling a man-made niche and each one offering intellectual justification for human excesses and lustful desires. The most contemporary cult chosen to reject Almighty God is "humanism" and its political offspring, modern liberalism. It has found "scientific" evidence in the theories of Darwin to reject God.

The various evolutionary "ideas" have been joyfully welcomed and sanctified by the latest batch of atheists, even though Charles Darwin, later in life, had cause to doubt his own speculation. Darwin's articulated ambivalence has not dampened the evangelical fervor and faith of his followers, nor have the recent discoveries of contemporary science destroyed the Darwinian thesis. Evolutionists still choose to believe for all the obvious reasons.

"Evolution" provides a "scientific" justification for rejecting the laws of God and ignoring the discipline inherent therein. Evolutionary humanism and modern radical liberalism releases mankind from fear of God's retribution, judgment, and eternal damnation. Humanistic logic justifies the rejection and abandonment of God's laws and thereby ignores the necessity of living by God's eternal laws. Unbelief, humanism, radical liberalism cast man adrift from the principles and foundation of Western civilization and bring into question the origin of all morals based on a Creator. Radical evolutionists believe that because man evolved, he, and he alone, is the alpha and omega of all morals—the creator of standards and all human values.

Ethics and morality, humanists insist, reflect contemporary thought and are the product of man's imagination and consensus. By humanist reasoning, ethics are also—like man—evolving. Thus, by humanist definition, there are no absolute standards, no immutable laws of conduct, no constant principles governing man's behavior. To put it in the contemporary vernacular, "Anything goes, baby, as long as you can get away with it."

Is it possible for a radical liberal to have a conscience, to feel guilt over telling a lie? Do they have pangs of remorse when being politically underhanded and forcing their will on others?

Not in the least. In fact, if lying advances their political goals, they conclude it's immoral not to lie. They latch on to an old Commie cliché, "The end justifies the means." If you accept the humanist perspective and especially the absence of God, why not?

Why bother to worry about a conscience if there is no God to hold us accountable? It can be argued that a conscience apart from God is impossible. What would constitute the foundation of one's conscience without God's laws? Are we capable of constructing a conscience on our own? Upon reflection, knowing the fallibility of man, that is highly improbable if not impossible.

Conservatives wonder why liberals aren't bothered by their consciences when they twist the truth, covet the wealth of others and get caught in a bald-faced lie. The reason is simple: one can't be bothered by what isn't there. Webster's dictionary defines conscience as, "Knowledge or sense of right and wrong, with a compulsion to do right."

Right and wrong by whose standards? God's or someone else's? A wealth of "intellectuals" have written volumes expanding upon the theme that God the Creator doesn't exist. They expound further that not only does He not exist, but belief in Him has been harmful to mankind. They lay the ills of the world at His feet.

Lenin contemptuously wrote of religion, "Religion teaches those who toil in poverty ... to be resigned and patient in this world, and consoles them with the hope of reward in heaven.... Religion is the opium of the people." Nice guy Lenin, a first-class humanist. The blood trail of suffering he left will be remembered for centuries.

The last century has seen a proliferation of such authors. This nihilistic "God-is-dead" idea has spawned numerous political and intellectual movements of monumental significance, including Marxist-Leninist communism, Fabian socialism, Hitler's National Socialist Party (NAZI), Benito Mussolini's fascism, the American socialist movement, the contemporary humanist and the hard leftist beatniks of the '60s. Judge Robert Bork describes the radicals definitively in his marvelous book,

Slouching Towards Gomorrah. For the serious student, this manuscript is must reading.

The differences between all of the aforementioned humanists are gossamer thin. If there is any distinction between them, it is the degree of force each one is willing to use in order to impose ideas on the "unwashed masses." Communists and Nazis pragmatically exterminated their opposition; contemporary humanists want to brainwash them into submission. In either case, all wish for total political power without dissenting opinions.

What, then, are the logical consequences of humanistic thought, and what behavior emanates from these assumptions? Is truth absolute? Are there ultimate rights and wrongs? The answer, for them, is obviously no. There are no absolute rights and wrongs; hence all ethical values are malleable, changeable, and somewhat irrelevant. *Ethics are situational; the situation dictates which ethics apply.*

To a liberal, the word hypocrisy doesn't exist. Caught in a falsehood or the evident failure of a policy, the "moral" thing for the liberal to do is extricate himself with the least amount of political damage. Any response is possible—deny, admit guilt, ask forgiveness, attack the character of the accuser—whatever works. If the opposition is incapable of exploiting the lie, ignore them—because if no political harm occurs, who cares?

Who then can change what constitutes public morals? Anyone with enough power to force others to obey!

A chilling example of the consequences of humanistic logic was the rationalization Ted Bundy used in justifying the murders of so many young women. Bundy, the serial killer, taped a conversation with one of his victims shortly before he murdered her. While a college student, Bundy had accepted the "logic" that all laws are man-made. Thus, he argued, he saw no reason why he, a man, couldn't arbitrarily change them. Killing gave him pleasure, so why not kill?

God and His immutable laws—to Ted Bundy and others of like mind—are nothing more than the figment of mankind's fertile imagination. God is a mythological character who has persisted throughout the ages, a placebo for the superstitious to adore or fear.

When one thinks about it, what is the intellectual difference between the premises of a Ted Bundy, Adolph Hitler, Mikhail Gorbachev, or a contemporary abortionist doctor? Bundy killed for his own pleasure, Hitler killed for the sake of the Aryan race, Gorbachev killed Afghans in the name of the Soviet State, and an abortionist kills for money or to eliminate a "mistake." Small difference to the dead.

To the humanists and contemporary liberals, all laws derived from the supernatural are flawed and in need of change. Adherence to such laws may even be immoral. As an example, no laws relating to sexual behavior—sodomy, homosexuality, incest, and any manner of perversity—are justifiable if those actions are viewed as nothing more than pleasurable sexual acts between animals. If the theory of evolution is true, and man is nothing more than a few steps above some prehistoric mud, what harm is there in performing sex acts between consenting parties of the same sex or from one beast to another? If pleasurable, who is to say it is wrong? Anyone for snake?

If we are all mere animals, who can say the rights of one animal exceed another? Putting any animal to death may be deemed a barbarous act if one equates all forms of life as having equal value. Conversely, if we are but animals, the taking of human life can be easily justified if some social good is achieved, such as the Chinese justifying their population control, the Nazis killing Jews, science "dignifying" the death of the elderly with poison, or a third-term abortion.

Saving the lives of dogs and cats while killing unborn humans may seem contradictory, but not if all standards are manmade. Any value can be formulated to fit any situation; all that is needed is to control the reins of power, the law-making bodies and the executive arm of government. Once in control, the humanists believe they have all the muscle necessary to dictate what constitutes the prevailing right or wrong.

Once gaining control of the centers of power, what do the humanists do? They act immediately and in all ways to maximize their own power. Therefore, the most consistent action of the humanist in power is the centralization of political power and the socialization of government. Local governments must be made subservient to state governments, which in turn are to be made subservient to the national government. Once this is accomplished, internationalizing becomes the goal, forming a one-world government where all human behavior can be manipulated, contrary beliefs can be eradicated, education totally controlled, and mankind "perfected."

This, of course, presupposes the "perfectors" know what they are doing. One is hardly comforted when one contemplates the Clintons, Kennedys, and the Barney Franks holding the ultimate reins.

It is easily understood why humanists gravitate to education, media, and government. They believe man is a malleable animal with no spiritual source of information or inspiration; thus, his brain is programmable. Like a computer, he can be systematically fed specific information that will control his behavior. They perceive most people as filled with religious trivia and possessing contaminated minds. They see education—controlling the source of information to the young—as the way to correct this condition by reprogramming them to be more "enlightened."

What then is moral to a humanist? Achieving the goals of control. What techniques are used? Whatever works!

Prevarication (deviating from or perverting the truth) becomes a tactic rather than a moral violation. If found out, bluff, plead ignorance, denounce the accuser, or even dialectically apologize by admitting the mistake, begging forgiveness, even promising restitution. *Lying, therefore, brings no pang of conscience. The error is in getting caught.*

It is important to note that all evolutionists/humanists are not in agreement about the implementation of their humanist society. They argue over the manner and degree as to how much force should be used to implement socialism. They do not argue over the necessity of state control or the fundamentals. Thus, the more brutal Communists never had qualms about wiping out whole populations to achieve their ends, while the "more gentle" socialists prefer indoctrination. Communists always found mass murder much more convenient than having to "re-educate" masses of mentally "contaminated" people. Much as a farmer kills a herd of anthrax-infected cattle, Communists have massacred Poles, Cambodians, Chinese, and Russians—more than 100 million people.

Although some humanists decry the brutality of Communism, they are still wedded to it by their mutual humanistic beliefs. American radical liberals are intellectually married to communists by the ideology of socialism, evolutionary theory and mutual goals. Their common enemy is Western civilization, specifically the American tradition. Many humanists consider themselves good Americans with a different idea on how the country should be managed. Labeling them "un-American" raises their hackles because they believe they have every right to advocate their ideas. Legally, they do. As long as they are not agents of a foreign government and are citizens of the United States, they can openly advocate what they jolly well please.

However, the consequences of socialist programs would completely obliterate the principles upon which this country was founded and usher in a totalitarian system every bit as corrupt as the one that existed in Russia.

Inherent within socialism is arbitrary force gravitating into the hands of the most evil of men. Corruption increases in direct proportion to the size of government and its centralization. This is because it is easier to hide evil within the labyrinth of agencies, commissions, and endless bureaus, especially if it is far removed from the governed. As in Gresham's economic law of bad money driving out good, bad bureaucrats force moral employees out of government, and it is they, the immoral, who rise to the top of the bureaucracy. This fact was marvelously stated in F. A. Hayek's classic, *The Road to Serfdom*.

American humanists, evolutionists, communists, socialists, and the extreme environmental leadership are all intellectual soul mates. What groups they join or what they call themselves should not cloud the issue. We should not be confused by the arguing and fighting they do among themselves, nor be comforted by it. It is a family fight over who should lead or how the socialization should take place.

The greatest murderers of the twentieth century—Hitler, Mao Tse-Tung, and Stalin—were socialists, humanists, and believers in evolution. Hitler joined Stalin to conquer Poland, then they fought each other. What about? Power—over who should rule!

It is also important to differentiate between the professional liberal and the amateurs who just mouth the cause. Those who financially profit from humanist liberalism have a vested interest in the growth and continuation of the intellectual pap they promote. Liberalism has paid off handsomely to those ensconced in the bowels of government. They have financial as well as ideological reasons for promoting the liberal myth; they owe their position to being willing advocates of humanistic doctrine. They advance up through the ranks because they are good soldiers, not independent thinkers. They also know they would soon be deposed should they start to advocate contrary beliefs.

It would be a mistake to believe that all who advocate the humanist line are ideologues, deeply committed to the cause and intellectually bound by its presuppositions. Many people can advocate a cause yet never understand the underlying reasons motivating the organizers. One can rattle off philosophic clichés with no knowledge of their origin or comprehension of the short-range, much less the long-range, significance of what is being promoted.

Visceral, gut feelings move a number of liberal advocates, especially the young. Benign parental intellectual neglect has created a vacuum that many humanist academics have readily filled, stuffing nonsense into young, inquiring minds. Students are ready receptacles for old totalitarian ideas wrapped in contemporary "humanitarian" cloth. Students are easily involved in a good-sounding cause when they lack the capacity or experience to understand its ultimate ramifications.

Promote a bad idea long enough and one often develops a vested interest in its continuation, becoming impervious to logic and common sense when one's ego is involved. Also, an individual can prosper, be accepted and admired for advocating a "just" humanist cause—even though he may later suspect the "cause" to be flawed. Reversing one's thinking, once doubts creep in, can be monetarily and socially very painful.

Individuals, even massive numbers of people, can be actors in a human drama without ever knowing the author of the play. Many can and do promulgate humanist ideas with no understanding that they're working contrary to their own best interests and that of others.

Often contradictory behavior appears in certain liberal individuals. They are self-professed agnostics who manifest a conscience and seemingly attempt to live "good" lives, even though they act with no understanding of the Christian origin of their moral premises. There are also churchgoers who promote humanist deeds without recognizing the apparent contradictions between their actions and their professed faith.

Few people take the time to seek out or study the genesis of their own beliefs, much less understand those who are their ideological opposition. But, those who attempt to understand *both* sides will affect the future of America.

There is a big difference between an author of a play and the performers who act out his imagination. How much more real is the drama when God writes the script—or more pathetic when man is the playwright.

3

The Liberal's Compromise: I Win, You Lose ... Then You Lose Some More

What occurs when these contradictory ideologies come into contact with one other, when those believing in traditional American concepts of limited government are assaulted by some new socialist program advanced by the liberals? Traditionalists, attempting to preserve the status quo, invariably and predictably react negatively.

It's important to know how each side views the confrontation—as a positive or a negative? Who gains, who loses? Traditional Americans dislike conflict and withdraw from it as a matter of habit and training. On the other hand, the humanists look upon confrontation as a necessity, a positive ingredient in advancing humanistic programs. They expect confrontation, plan for it and anticipate the predictable, negative reaction from their opposition, often using the reaction to further promote their cause. *Conflict, therefore, is expected, welcomed, analyzed, and then used to advance their goals.*

Momentum is obviously on the side of the aggressors since they have the tactical advantage of initiating the attack. Before their intended opposition even knows a clash will occur, they've had the opportunity to plan strategy, organize support, select the field of battle, choose the appropriate time to launch the new program, and frame the issue in such a manner as to put their program in the best light. *(More on framing the issue in the next chapter.)* They know opposition will be forthcoming, since their plans are usually expensive, assault the Constitution, and will enlarge the bureaucracy. All three are anathema to the traditionalist.

The humanist knows that how a program is presented often determines the outcome. Propaganda-wise, they wrap the socialist "idea" in a semantic blanket of sophistry, warm-cuddly humanitarianism, designed to put the opposition on the defensive.

Without question, the aggressor has the immediate advantage.

As they launch the conflict, the leftists anticipate the opposition's response and estimate their effectiveness. The issue is pursued until the conservative resistance becomes formidable and an overall negative result could occur. At that time, a dialectic, backward step is in order; a strategic retreat, giving up some ground.

The liberals then offer a partial solution in the form of a compromise. Half, instead of the whole loaf, is demanded. The left suddenly creates the aura of appearing reasonable, moderating their request. Leftist dialectics include planned retreats, a tactic used to confuse and throw the opposition off-guard. Lenin called it an important tool in accomplishing Communism's overall goals.

He used the analogy of a man driving a nail with a hammer, the backward stroke being just as important as the forward thrust of hitting the nail.

Liberal strategists ask for much more than they expect to gain immediately and then, when opposition builds, give in a little, play the good guy willing to concede. Switch from bad guy to good guy, be conciliatory, be sweetness and light, offer "compromise." Initiate the conflict, then strategically back off.

Consider the bandit who sticks a gun in your ribs and demands your wallet. Then with a kindly smile he gives back your credit cards saying, "Shucks, I don't really need these." Then he adds, "Aw, heck, I don't need these either," and returns the children's snapshots and the wallet itself—minus the cash, of course. Later, you tell the police he wasn't such a bad guy after all.

Most Americans will accept compromise in order to avoid a continuation of the confrontation. When the left backs off, a sigh of relief is usually heard from the traditionalists. In fact, the weakest and least informed on left-wing tactics often dictate the terms of how much is lost, since the timid are the ones usually intimidated and most anxious to see the hostilities end. In hopes of maintaining some of the status quo, this weakest link usually decides the amount surrendered and justifies acceptance with a begrudging, "We can live with that."

So, can the lamb live with the lion? He can—until the lion becomes hungry again.

The humanists accept the "compromise," having gained some ground—not all that they ultimately wanted, but more than they had before the confrontation began. Once the "compromise" takes place, the status quo side happily retires from the fight, slightly disgruntled over the loss of territory but relieved that the conflict is over.

The leftists immediately take to the media, railing against the compromise forced upon them by the heartless, self-seeking traditionalists.

The camel's nose—and likely all of his neck—is under the tent.

The left, with more recruits in their ranks and a foothold gained, patiently awaits the opportune time to start anew with more demands for more territory. This has been referred to as the "salami" technique, one slice at a time until everything is consumed. This is the way socialism has penetrated the body politic of America: one slice at a time, a large step forward and then a small step backward. Lenin stated it best: "We advance through retreat."

It's unfortunate that there is only one definition for the word "compromise." There should be two: one for defining the many physical compromises we all make as a matter of daily living, and the other for compromising of principle.

Let me give you an example of the differences between the two. My wife and I decide to rent a movie. She wants a love-'em-up, and I want a shoot-'em-up. Instead, to make us both happy, we rent a comedy. We both "compromised" our first desire and settled on a movie we both could enjoy. No principle was involved, just a physical giving-in, each watering down a personal choice in order to maintain family harmony. All of us do this daily—especially if we want to stay married.

Compare this with a compromise of principle.

I support the Second Amendment, believing all law-abiding Americans have a right to own firearms. The left believes in the confiscation of all firearms, especially handguns. What compromise can there be between us? Any infringement on this right is a loss to Americans. As you can see, there is no "physical" common ground. By definition, compromise is a settlement of differences with mutual concessions being made by both parties. This is how the dictionary defines the word. Both sides give up something.

This is not how the leftists "compromise." They will ask for 100 percent, then give in a little on their outlandish demands when opposition becomes formidable. They may call it compromise, but what are they giving up? Absolutely nothing! In order to implement their humanist agenda, are they sacrificing anything? Are they relinquishing control or perhaps abandoning some other established bureaucracy in order to negotiate in good faith? Never. They relinquish nothing while insisting we compromise away a piece of our freedom.

When we object, they have the unmitigated gall to say we're not reasonable. When we strenuously resist, they call us names—extreme, right-wing, ultra-conservative, and worse. Unfortunately, we react angrily, instead of calmly insisting they put something of equal or greater value on the table. When the socialists promote more socialized medicine, does anyone stand up and ask, "In exchange for more control of medicine, what are you liberals willing to give up—the EPA (Environmental Protection Agency)? OSHA (Occupational and Safety Health Administration)? Welfare? What are you willing to concede?"

Such a question is rarely, if ever, posed by the conservative. No one seems to think of it. When we give in to liberals, even an inch, we're not compromising; we're abdicating our rights and our honor. When our legislators do likewise, they are abdicating our rights and their honor.

We must stop using the term "compromise" when confronting the left. It should not be a part of our vocabulary when dealing with the left unless we ask the question, "What are you putting on the table in exchange? HUD (Housing and Urban Development)? ATF (Bureau of Alcohol, Tobacco, Firearms, and Explosives)? NEA (National Education Association)?"

We must put the picture in proper perspective. We're not out to rewrite our United States Constitution, abandon our freedoms, or force our ideas on anyone—but they are. We Americans like the way our forefathers put this nation together. We are, by definition, protectors of the status quo form of government bequeathed to us by our Founders. And why not? It's well worth maintaining.

When you think about it, all we ask is to have the same rights and privileges that our forefathers had and to have the same Constitutional protections they enjoyed.

The problem is that this position is a defensive one while the advantage favors those advocating change. The left takes the time to draft the issue in the best possible terms, estimate the level of opposition and pick an advantageous time to launch their plan of action. They certainly have nothing to lose. For should they fail, they are no worse off than when they started. When they obtain only a small portion of what they originally demanded, they are still ahead of the game.

Just think of all the socialist programs they have implemented—one step at a time. They advocate, we defend, and confrontation ensues. Then, the traditionalists are asked to "compromise." In order to see the hostilities end, we concede a little. Later, we concede a little more until all is gone.

There can be no compromises with the left. We are ideologically at opposite ends of the spectrum with no arbitration possible. Either they win or we do. They will run the government or we will. That's the only choice open to either of us. They know it—shouldn't we?

The time has come for us to start asking for the abolition of certain government agencies. Then, if we must, we can "compromise" and see only half of them disappear—this year. Before this can be accomplished, we need effective control of the legislative process.

The average American tends to see the participants in all these leftist "causes" as well-meaning folks trying to do some good. They see each cause as a separate effort, with no central theme or network linking them together. Only when viewed as an overall movement to centralize and expand government does it make sense. Then the puzzle fits together. The various causes may appear to have nothing in common. Why would macho labor unions back candidates who are pro-homosexual? What can be the tie between the abortionists and the anti-gun movement—what causes seem to be further apart?

Yet these quiet coalitions have been the backbone of liberal success for decades.

The reason is that the agendas for people-control are identical. Both advocate more government and support similar candidates for office. The preponderance of their leadership are, for all intents and purposes, ideological soul mates, social reformers, hard-leftists of the first order, invariably imbued with situational ethics and humanist ideals. They are out to change America by demanding more and then settling for less—one chunk at a time.

4

Humanist Organization and Planned Confrontation on the Path to Liberal Power

Humanists do not sit idle, waiting for the country to fall into their laps. They aren't blessed with broad public support for the substance of their socialist boondoggles. They've had to incrementally impose their nutty ideas on Americans. In order to do that, they have had to formulate, subvert, gravitate to, or capitalize on special areas of public interest to help their movement grow. They either exploit or manufacture causes in order to advance socialism. The humanists' goal is to gain total power. They need vehicles to achieve this end. They carefully choose an existing issue or create one, then organize a given class of citizenry around it. *The cause is of secondary importance. The primary concern is the organizational possibilities.*

The subject in question must contain certain criteria to be worth the effort. It must have a long life for the purpose of properly developing the issue. This is called "shelf life." Like fruit, the cause must be able to last long enough on the shelf before it loses its potency. The project cannot decay or suddenly disappear. Sufficient time is needed to put the project together, frame the issue in the most favorable light, recruit followers and build the aura of public support.

The object is usually to garner a populist imagery to justify governmental intervention. *I stress the word imagery because real, tangible support is not necessarily needed; just the perception of popular support will suffice.*

Usually, humanist legislation is already waiting in the wings, ready for introduction by leftists previously placed in office. The object, of course, is to justify the creation of a new government program or expand an old one. Bureaucratic employment will then be provided for their followers, thereby broadening their base and further legitimizing their cause. This also creates more public employee union dollars for their political action committees, funneling major funds into the election of more of their own kind and incrementally advancing their humanist goals.

What are the criteria needed to organize effective "causes" or (as some of these used to be known) "front groups"? The issue selected should have:

- A sizeable universe of potential followers in order to make the organizational effort worthwhile.
- A hard core of knowledgeable, trained spokesmen and leaders.
- Enough seed money to carry the project until sufficient funds can be raised from new supporters (or the taxpaying public).
- Ongoing professional management to keep their issue propaganda before the public.
- A medium through which to rally support; either mail, email, or with existing print, TV, or radio spots.

For example, the environmental issue is a natural for the left to use, it having all the right ingredients: a large naïve public, a gullible, sympathetic liberal press, a confrontationally illiterate business community to blame, and the "motherhood" issue of saving America and the world from contamination and ruin. The subject is emotional and easily manipulated because negative statistics can be readily conjured up out of thin air or manufactured by legions of government-paid researchers (either government employees or feeders on the government research-grant gravy train), along with half-truths on impending environmental doom. Data disproving alleged problems are usually difficult to acquire, confusing, and all-but-ignored by the major media.

Once accused of eco-contamination, the business community is guilty until proven innocent. Besides, how many of us can actually prove or disprove global warming, the thickness of the ozone layer, or rarity of a given bug? Environmental extremists can claim or disclaim almost anything they want, with little fear of repercussions.

Let me give a small example that perfectly illustrates what I am talking about. A number of years ago, California animal rights activists claimed the mountain lion was endangered and demanded a moratorium on hunting this beast of prey. The puma is a nocturnal, secretive predator, rarely seen during daylight hours. Establishing data verifying its numbers took years of research by California's Department of Fish and Game. As it turned out, there was an abundance of these predatory animals, but that was not discovered before the anti-hunting animal rights activists had their way. They called for a moratorium on hunting the mountain lion and got what they wanted from left-leaning legislators.

I was a member of the California State Senate Natural Resources Committee that heard testimony on the moratorium legislation. One college professor emphatically stated, "My research shows the mountain lion is in danger of extinction!" I had the gall to ask him to explain how his research was conducted and pressed him for a straight answer. He was unbelievably evasive but finally admitted his scientific research amounted to seating students in the back of his car, driving backcountry byways and looking for pug marks. That was it! Paw prints by the side of the road! The liberals on the committee were in the majority and accepted the professor's drivel as proof.

Of course, the moratorium negatively impacted hunting, thus substantially affecting gun ownership. The number of mountain lions increased rapidly, thereby reducing the deer population dramatically. Hunting licenses fell precipitously as the deer herds shrank, causing a continual diminishment in hunters and the purchase of hunting firearms.

With less natural feed, predator impact on domestic livestock increased, as well as attacks on humans. Not long ago, two young women were killed and eaten by lions. Do you think the left then advocated we return to the hunting of these predators because of the loss of human life and livestock? Not a chance. In fact, the attempt to lift the moratorium was vociferously fought.

The left has tried to make the "environment" practically everyone's concern. Normal anxieties over its protection have been exploited and used effectively by leftist bureaucrats. They see it as a marvelous vehicle to socialize property while employing tens of thousands of environmental studies graduates who were matriculated from the liberal temples of higher learning.

Again, it must be stated that the "issue" can be of little consequence to the socialist organizers. A prize example happened during World War II. The British Communists organized a movement to obtain coal for housewives, hoping to recruit new devotees. In short order they succeeded in delivering the coal. However, they considered this particular action a failure even though their professed "goal" had been achieved. There had not been sufficient time to recruit, agitate, and educate the housewives on the benefits of Communism. There were no residual benefits from the effort, so they deemed the project a waste of time. The Communists were not interested in the coal for the housewives, they merely used it as a vehicle to organize and advance Communism. The cause was of secondary importance, if important at all.

For conservatives, the cause is all-important. However, the organizational advantages open to them for recruitment, education, and long-range political goals rarely cross their minds. They react, do battle, and then disband, perceiving each struggle as a separate entity. Not the left; they build on every engagement, knowing full well the present effort is but one engagement in a protracted conflict, a fight that will take decades to win completely.

The humanists believe that any political battle where a residual is not gained, new converts attained, or some part of the program implemented, is a waste of time, energy, money, and manpower. They are absolutely correct. Meanwhile, too many conservatives meet, eat, and retreat—building no residuals, gaining no new allies, and putting no money in the bank for the political fights that will surely come next.

When leftists launch confrontation, no particular leftist group operates alone. They network with each other and call for assistance in pressuring the legislature to act. These seemingly divergent structures add their weight to the cause, creating an impression of broad public support.

The liberally inclined media, given a more-than-ample amount of one-sided data, help propagandize to the public that a real problem exists and then recommend a government solution. Whether to save the trees ... owls ... seals ... or house the homeless, the issue is articulated in a manner that automatically puts any opposition on the defensive. Being against these so-called good causes is perceived as heartless, selfish, and right-wing extremism. The people hired by government will inevitably come from the advocates of the leftist cause. Why? Because they will claim that they are the only ones who understand the complexities of the problem and are trained to solve it.

Leftists are masters of creating support groups out of thin air, especially when needed to testify before legislative committees or at press conferences. These groups, who reportedly speak for the masses, are rarely questioned about their membership size, financing, or history. Most Republican legislators are usually too polite or gullible to bore in or question their credentials. The industry under attack rarely thinks to investigate these advocate bodies who conveniently appear before committees. The average liberal-leaning reporter does not care. If penetrating questions are asked of these groups regarding their membership, finances, or the length of time they have been in existence, the leftists on the committee invariably come to their defense. If a liberal legislator chairs the committee, the humanist witnesses are the first on the docket to testify. The TV cameras and press cover their lengthy testimony and then disappear in order to make deadlines, usually before the opposition can say anything to the contrary.

These dog-and-pony shows are commonplace around every state capitol and the Congress, especially when left-wing

Democrats control the committee membership. The votes are already pre-ordained and counted before the committee even convenes to hear testimony. The actual committee discussion is for the press and cameras, nothing but planned propaganda. The whole show is to make the process look democratic and palatable to the public.

The leftist legislators are part of the orchestration, not objective representatives trying to assess facts in order to form learned conclusions. The ducks are lined up in advance and the committee hearings are nothing more than a part of the schmoozing process, the verbal gamesmanship used to create a veneer of respectability for the impending legislation. Witnesses unfamiliar with how the game is played are chewed up in these hearings and pilloried by the liberals. I have witnessed presidents of large corporations cringe before senators and assemblymen, legislators unfit to carry their dirty laundry.

To the average citizenry, confrontation is not perceived as a tactic, a method of achieving a given end—to liberals, it is. *They view the act of confrontation as a verbal game, a form of semantic warfare to achieve a specific end, a strategy of bluff and bluster, a tactic used to accomplish a political goal, a technique to put an opponent on the defensive.*

Because confrontation is not understood as a tactic, average Americans are manipulated by those who are practitioners of the art. Humanistic liberalism uses confrontational methodology as a very successful political weapon. Most Americans don't know humanism exists, much less understand the ramifications of its philosophy and methodology.

This behavior confuses the average citizen who has been raised under the influence of religious morals. By applying his own set of standards to a controversial situation, the citizen is taken advantage of … *he becomes a victim of his own decency.* He would never do to others as was done to him. When attempting to be fair and reasonable, he is verbally assaulted and pilloried. When he makes a small concession, more is demanded. Only when he angrily organizes an effective defense does the opposition negotiate and offer to back off a little. He then breathes a sigh of relief now that the left seems willing to be reasonable and negotiate. When the "compromise" is reached, the traditional American is emotionally exhausted—and relieved that the confrontation is over. Meanwhile, the humanist has already begun to organize for another attack, planning to slice himself another piece of the pie.

Conservative activists must not be fooled by this dialectic tactic or taken in by the liberals' move to lessen some of their exorbitant demands. *Remember, the liberal only backs off when he has to; he retreats only out of necessity.* He watches the pressure build, and when it reaches a level that can do him harm, only then will he step back on any of his demands.

When the liberals step dialectically backward, the conservative attack must be intensified, not diminished. We must use the animosity the left has provoked to continue to expand our conservative organization and leverage their programs into oblivion.

We must never forget that in practice socialism fails. With every new leftist program, somebody's ox will be gored, barbecued, and fricasseed, offering the conservative marvelous opportunities to organize the angry and translate that animosity into positive confrontation. A number of conservative organizations have succeeded in fighting the radical left by wisely organizing minorities of gored voters. Gun Owners of California and Gun Owners of America are two good examples. The attacks upon gun ownership made possible the organization of an effective political structure, causing the defeat of many anti-gun legislators. Other conservative groups could and should do the same around other issues.

What have we learned from the above? Perhaps a candle has been lit. In subsequent chapters we will attempt to show how this information can be used to our advantage. As Sun Tsu wisely advised, "Know thy enemy as well as thyself."

5

Elites, Power, and Politics— What is Leadership?

An FBI undercover agent, who had infiltrated the American communist movement, related how he recruited college students for the Party. In a two-year period, he identified twenty-two young students who wanted to be part of the cadre. One evening, he and his superiors met to go over the list of eager new recruits. Much to his surprise, they culled all but three. He asked curiously, "Why select only three after all that hard work?"

His superior answered, "Comrade, one in the right place is all we need."

Reflecting on that account and contemplating the written words of Lenin, one realizes Lenin didn't need or want large numbers, only a select few. He desired to build "the dictatorship of the proletariat," the ruling elite, from the small percentage who grasped the abstracts of politics. Lenin believed that only a small minority of leftist intellectuals was necessary to take over the world. He wished to recruit only those elitists capable of understanding and adhering to Marxist-Leninist dogma and tactics. Lenin understood that increasing numbers would bog down the movement and be diluted by those who didn't intellectually grasp the need for a dedicated, well-organized, philosophically driven hard core.

How right he was. Communist membership swelled to over seven percent in Russia and turned into a privileged bureaucracy, which fell of its own weight.

Lenin clearly recognized that only a small percentage of any nation had a sense and an understanding for political abstracts and the ability to act upon that knowledge. He believed in leverage, that a small number properly placed could lead the masses. If he could put together a loyal revolutionary cadre and subvert political structures, his comrades could have disproportionate leverage and eventually gain power.

He was mechanically right on two points. Only a few people do think politically, and a small cadre of dedicated zealots can take over an entire country because their targets did not know how to oppose them. It took less than a hundred followers to subvert the millions in Czarist Russia.

Lenin also understood the mechanical need to promote socialism because it centralizes governmental power. Centralized government makes it easier to subvert. Socialism was, and still is, a necessary precursor to eventual totalitarian domination of the world.

Decentralized governments, where public power is widely dispersed and the citizens have maximum personal liberty, are infinitely more difficult for a minority to subvert and control. Lenin called the masses, "asses, malleable putty," in need of management by their intellectual superiors. Marxist-Leninist ideology was, and still is, an elitist intellectual movement. Although severely damaged by Russian failures, communist dogma still controls the thoughts and actions of billions of people and an inordinate number of tenured college professors.

Bad ideas don't die of their own accord; they have to be killed by better ones. History shows large numbers of intellectuals can have a vested interest in ignorance. The world has suffered over a hundred years of Marxist-Leninist dogma to prove the point. For many years, we have seen how such small numbers of elitists, with organization and dedication, can implement a malignant philosophy; especially when good ideas are taken for granted and languish.

Before the turn of the twentieth century, socialist mythology had gained a serious hold amongst the intellectuals of Europe and was systematically infecting America as well. Socialist promises sounded so nice and comfy. The Industrial Revolution was in full swing. Newly acquired wealth and personal freedom were slowly being taken for granted while socialism, the antithesis of liberty, was being sold as security for all.

Lenin wasn't the only one who recognized that just a small percentage of the population thinks politically or acts upon that knowledge. Fabian socialists in England and Adolph Hitler's followers acted on that same assumption.

In America, statistics show that less than 5 percent of the registered voters actively participate within the fabric of politics (e.g., political participation beyond voting). Within that small number, there is an even smaller percentage that comprises the leadership of both liberal and conservative activists. Within these tiny percentages, the fate of the nation resides.

To prove the point, consider the old adage, "Put your money where your mouth is." It tells a good story. A person's political intensity is obvious when we see how much he will spend. The average American will happily spend fifty to one hundred dollars dining out with his family. But ask him to contribute twenty-five dollars to a candidate, and you'd think he'd been asked to repay the national debt.

Less than 2 percent of the nation's registered voters voluntarily contributes money to candidates.

In California, a very politically active state, only a minute percentage of the registered voters participates beyond voting. Combine all of the active Democrats, Independents, Republicans, door-to-door walkers, precinct captains, campaign headquarter workers, left wing, right wing, no wing; combine everyone, and you have much less than 5 percent of the registered voters participating in the selection of their government. The percentages are much smaller when you factor in all those who don't even register to vote.

The activists produce the candidates and do the work of campaigning; the voters just pick someone already selected for them. It is easy to understand why most liberals are elitists. They look upon most people as non-participating political dumb-dumbs, dolts, little people in need of guidance from the cradle to grave. They are right about needing good political leadership, but not from those who want to play God with them.

We are all better off when liberty is optimized and each citizen is self-reliant. We are all dumb about some things and smart about others. People are not stupid just because they don't grasp the complexities of—or are not interested in—daily politics. We all have different levels of knowledge based upon our God-given talents. In His infinite wisdom, we are created individually unique, blessed with varied skills, interests, and activities.

We must recognize the diversity amongst people and applaud it, not condemn it, and acknowledge that we are all unequal and be thankful. Only through our inequality of talents do we have something to offer one another. Wouldn't it be horrible if we were all alike—all "equal"? Perish the thought. We are equal only in the eyes of God, each with inalienable rights. But in talent or ability? No way! We are all unequal with a diversification of abilities granted to each of us.

Aren't we all delighted that some choose to excel in the healing arts? When our children are ill, do we want them cared for by an equal-opportunity medicine man? I think not. We want the best, the most unequal doctor available. We can hardly fault an excellent physician who knows little about politics but gives his spare time freely to healing the poor. Don't we all benefit by other individuals striving for excellence? The answer is obvious.

The rub comes when one is gifted in a given field, but then believes that talent allows him to lord it over others in different disciplines. The doctor may feel he's superior to a garage mechanic, but what good is his medical talent when his car is broken down and he's stranded on some lonely road?

"Elitism" is a common malady that affects many, especially those afflicted with an affinity for politics. Leftist humanists see themselves as superior because they have a deep interest in the workings of politics. This messianic complex translates itself into a desire to run and regulate everything and everyone, from the scientist to the farmer, the educator to the janitor. This justification to rule others is aided by an aphrodisiac—police power. Controlling the brute force of arbitrary government is heady stuff indeed, the most corrupting and harmful influence in the history of man.

6

How and Why
Ideological Minorities
Make Policy

The most insidious misconceptions are often half-truths. Within some factual statement an important part is conveniently ignored, creating a false impression. This is like the Hollywood producer who bragged that *The New York Times* had called his latest movie "colossal" when, in fact, the *Times* critic had dubbed it a "colossal flop!"

Democracy! Majorities elect! This conjures up the imagery that the preponderance of the citizenry elect their leadership but, in reality, it's a half-truth, a false assumption with major consequences. *The truth is that organized minorities elect—always have, and probably always will.*

Most Americans have little or nothing to do with establishing national policy because they don't participate in the selection of the candidates who ultimately make policy; a minority of voters do by voting in a party primary or convention.

Consider the following. There are more than 300 million people in the United States. Of these, 216 million are qualified to register to vote, but only about 142 million bother to register even in the hotly contested 2004 presidential election—less than half of the overall population. In 2004, only 126 million actually voted.

In the all-important primary races where the party nominee is selected, less than 50 percent of those registered trouble themselves to go to the polls. See how the numbers shrink? From 300 million to 216 million to 142 million to 126 million. In primaries there are usually multiple candidates, thereby splitting the vote even more for the winner. In 1992, several Democrats sought the presidential nomination. Bill Clinton won the primary with about 10 million votes; that's only 4 percent of the American population or only 6 percent of those who are qualified to vote. Six out of every one hundred adult Americans chose Clinton in 1992 as the Democrat's presidential candidate. Some mandate—some majority!

The numbers shrink even further when it comes to the all-important congressional and state legislative races. Judging by the public's participation, we can surmise that the majority of Americans don't seem to give a hoot about what their state senators and congressmen do. That too, is a half-truth. Americans do care; many just don't think their vote matters for much.

The important point is that there is a dramatic fall-off in the number of people who vote from the top of the ticket—president, governor, U.S. senator—to the seats below—Congress, state senate, etc. The fall-off gives a greater leverage position to those who do cast a ballot and an even greater impact for those who direct and influence a sizable number of votes.

Let me give you a classic example. In the '60s, the California Democrats artfully gerrymandered the state, creating more elective opportunities for their party. But, in order to create more Democrat than Republican seats, they had to cram as many registered Republicans as possible into several districts. In one of those heavy-Republican areas, they expected a particularly ineffective Republican assemblyman to seek one of the new state senate seats, but at the last moment he decided to stay in the assembly. There was a mad rush of Republican candidates seeking this office because the primary victor would easily win the General Election. Eight candidates sought the Republican nomination.

There were roughly 600,000 people in the district, of which 400,000 could have registered to vote, but only 235,000 bothered. In this all-important primary, 120,000 cast ballots—70,000 Republican, 50,000 Democrat. The Republicans split the 70,000 eight ways. The winning candidate polled 16,000 votes. It was called a landslide victory because the victorious Republican won with a 6,000-vote margin over his closest opponent. That's 16,000 ballots out of 400,000 potential voters—a landslide?

The 16,000 constituted a tiny fraction of those eligible to vote—4 percent! That small number selected the Republican candidate who went on to win the senate seat. That new senator was yours truly—"Landslide Richardson." I then served 22 years in the state senate.

Is this a rare, strange set of circumstances? No. It happens all the time. Let's walk through the figures once more:

Constituents:	600,000
Eligible to register:	400,000
Actually registered:	235,000
Primary election turnout:	120,000
Republican ballots cast:	70,000 (split eight ways)
Winner received:	16,000 (landslide victory)

To be perfectly candid, who do you think had my loyalty and comprised my "real constituency"? Guess whose opinions counted? The 600,000 who resided in the district, most of whom didn't vote for me? Or those who won the primary for me? How about the opinion of the 500 volunteers who worked in my campaign or the 100 hard-core who did most of the work? Guess which phone calls I returned and which were handled by staff? Legislators, both conservative and liberal, are far more loyal to their "real" constituencies than is generally understood.

The majority of elected officials know how the system works, which constituent deserves the friendly strokes and who gets the brush off. As an example, a congressman was being harangued by a waitress over an issue dear to her heart, not his. She wouldn't let up. The legislator was slightly inebriated and sorely irritated. Finally, he interrupted her diatribe, cocked one eyebrow and asked, "Are you registered to vote?"

Sticking out her chin she haughtily replied, "No, I'm not!"

"Well then, buzz off. Your opinion doesn't count."

Crude as it was, he was right. Her opinion didn't mean beans.

Races won by such small numbers are not uncommon. It happens all the time. We are not dealing with majorities, but minorities of voters who cast ballots at key times. Once elected, the left applies the same principle within the legislature. They can, and do, control the legislature with a minority as well.

Conservatives must also grasp the concept of leveraging the majority by being a minority; it doesn't take 50 percent plus one to call the tune. In most cases, the hard leftists are a minority within the legislative hall, but they know how to manage the entire body by creating the structure for control. The following is how it works in many states and within Congress.

Let's say, for example, the state assembly (the lower house) is made up of one hundred legislators. In this body there are fifty-one Democrats and forty-nine Republicans. Since the Democrats have the majority, they have the votes to select who will be the Speaker and other leadership posts. The liberal Democrats control leadership within their caucus because out of the fifty-one Democrats, twenty-six of them are hard-core liberals. Working together, the left controls the Democrat Caucus and thereby selects who the leaders will be. The Democrats then vote as a bloc and select the radicals by straight party line vote. Then, the Speaker selects the committee chairmen and committee membership. The Democrats get a majority on all-important committees such as Finance, Reapportionment, Judiciary, and Revenue and Tax. In order to be "fair," Republicans are given the chairmanship and majority membership of the Swamp Overflow Committee and Commission on Historical Cemeteries and Landmarks.

So, with only twenty-six, a fourth of the overall membership, the left-wing Democrats leverage the remaining seventy-four members. Joining with their outside pressure groups, the leftists maintain more than enough political clout on the moderate to conservative Democrats to keep them in line and prevent them from forming alliances with the Republicans. Leadership allows the liberals to control party funds, staff hiring, legislation, the key committees, thereby controlling the overall direction of the legislature.

What's to stop the good guys from doing the same? The shoe can fit the right foot as well as the left. Although a minority, confrontationally-trained conservatives could do the same in the Republican Party. If, within the Republicans, the most active were confrontationally motivated and organized (which they usually are not), great gains could be made.

It must be stressed, we are not talking about taking over all of Congress, only impacting a percentage of the existing body. Again, small numbers come into play. One doesn't have to move a fulcrum very far to change the leverage factor. A mere percentage change in the conservative Republicans in Congress could exercise immense leverage.

This is what the moral traditional Americans used to be—the salt of the earth—adding flavor, preserving truth, changing the taste of politics—movers of the fulcrum. We need not be the majority to change the political direction of America. The liberals have done it with a minority. Why can't we?

Can you imagine the changes in education, the social services, appropriations, the judiciary, agriculture, and commerce if morally confrontational, motivated men and women sat as the committee chairs? The positive changes that would occur boggle the mind.

By utilizing and understanding the principle of a leveraged minority, the hard-left has systematically gained control. They laugh at the "politically unwashed" majority. Remember, Lenin called the masses "asses." He, like our humanists, is wrong. The "masses" might not know much about politics, but that hardly makes them appropriate objects of contempt. Will Rogers put it succinctly, "We're all ignorant, but just about different things."

We may bemoan the lack of civic knowledge, but why bother? It is not productive to wail over how people behave. It is our job to understand them and take advantage of the present circumstances, not curse the civic darkness that prevails. If only a minority of voters cast ballots for the lower offices, then let's light a candle, make sure the majority of these minority votes are for the good guys. The leftists have understood this phenomenon, exploited it, and elected a lot of their own kind. There's nothing denying us the same opportunity.

Instead of damning the public, we should give them moral leadership. Important as it is to comprehend why people vote, it is more important to know why they don't. The reasons are varied but somewhat discernible. With some, they think there's not a "dime's difference" between both parties. So, why bother? Others believe their one vote makes no ripple in the sea of politics. Sometimes, it is not knowing enough about the candidates and not wanting to make a mistake. They feel sufficiently informed about the top of the ticket due to extensive media coverage but not enough about the lower offices, so they leave the rest of the ballot blank, hoping more informed voters will make the right choice.

Often, the voter is turned off, disgusted by the negative ads from both parties, and uses that as an excuse not to vote at all. For the same reason, a surprising number of citizens don't even register to vote. When marking a ballot, many vote for the lesser offices only as an afterthought, their attention focused on the presidential and gubernatorial candidates. In this case, they often split their tickets. For the lower offices, they accept the recommendations of their party, labor union, and friends, or are swayed by the suggestions of local media. This is particularly true in the absence of any other criteria, when voting for the "other offices."

I must stress this absence of any other criteria. Everyone has a pecking order as to what influences our vote or causes us to register in the first place. What do I mean by pecking order? It's the order of importance used in deciding who shall be chosen as our representatives. The pecking order varies with each individual, but the following fits many:

- Knowing the candidate personally
- Hot button issue
- Party registration
- Ethnic considerations

- Friend's recommendations
- Union affiliation and recommendation

The number one reason of importance is having a friendly relationship and access to an officeholder. This can be, and usually is, the reason certain people are elected in small constituencies. They personally know a lot of the people in the community and, combined with the exceedingly low voter turnout for local elections and absence of any organized opposition, the best known usually wins. Personal knowledge and friendship outweigh most other considerations. With larger constituencies, such as a congressional district (600,000+ people), the candidate can't possibly know a large percentage of the electorate. With larger constituencies, the four Ms come into play—money, management, manpower, and moxie. The last, the most important M, is knowing what to do and when to do it.

Once the voting habits of a district are carefully studied, an estimate can be made from past election statistics of the likely number of votes needed to win. Every district has voters who consistently cast their ballots. Among those are citizens who will change their vote if given a good reason.

The average voter feels little compulsion to seek out a candidate's qualifications—most wouldn't know where to begin anyway. They feel that the literature received, the TV ads, the recommendations of the local newspaper, the advice of friends, or party affiliation suffice. Most Americans wait to be wooed. Often, it never occurs to them that they should expend some extra energy to find out the good from the bad.

One good woman stated that she took the literature received from all the candidates, put it in a drawer and the day before the election, read it all—then decided. She thought she was being a good citizen. Compared to most, she was. She was pro-life, had impeccable pro-family values, was an active Christian, and wound up voting for a left-wing Democrat. No one had contacted her about his background and pointed out the dramatic differences between what he said in a campaign brochure and how he really felt. Whose fault was that? Hers? Not really. If there is any blame, it should be the lack of a conservative organization to inform her of the candidate's true position.

In the primaries, especially in the open seats where there is no incumbent running, most of these important state and Congressional elections are initially won by a candidate backed by some special interest group, or a network of such organizations. Victory belongs to those who organize the best and turn out the small number needed to win. The question is—which special interest group or organized minority wins? Theirs or ours? The black hats or the good guys? Somebody is going to win, and it might as well be one of us.

We must forget Civics 101, where we learned that public opinion affects national policy and the majority vote wins. It sounds good in theory, but it has little to do with reality. The politically active humanist knows better. So should we. The left is the first to stack the deck whenever the occasion arises. Once elected and in the majority, they gleefully gerrymander district lines to increase their advantage. They register voters at welfare offices, use dues forced from union membership to turn out the vote, politicize causes, and organize everyone from homosexuals to tree huggers.

The leftists have gained influence, but not by appealing to the masses or caring what the public thinks. They've gained power by systematically, methodically organizing various segments of the population, gaining control of some local governments, school boards, city councils, then state legislatures, then Congress, all by controlling a minority of the vote. Once in office, they leverage the office, use it for propaganda and fundraising, and work diligently to elect others of like mind. What we see today is the culmination of years of hard work by those of the socialist persuasion. They have foisted on us concepts alien and detrimental to our American culture and heritage. They have embedded their silly, unworkable ideas into the law, our educational institutions, and the media.

You've got to give the buggers credit—they've done a good job of screwing up the country, retaining power, and telling us we love it. They even have the nerve to tell us their programs fail because we, the taxpayers, haven't given them enough money to properly support their socialist boondoggles. In the name of liberty, they've denied liberty. In the hyperbole of freedom for all, they've immersed us into a cesspool of regulation and bureaucracy.

In the name of racial equality they have so divided Americans that hatred is the norm in many of our cities and schools. Do the leftists really want racial harmony, or do they prefer the existing acrimony? One must admit that the division has kept minorities as a Democrat voting bloc and helped sustained their power.

Let's face it, the leftists have gained power through the elective process, and if they lose it, it must be by the same method. That will occur only when traditional Americans organize, wise up, and recognize how they've been politically molested.

Abe Lincoln was somewhat right when he said, "You can fool some of the people all of the time and all of the people some of the time, but you can't fool all of the people all of the time."

But I say, if you can turn out some of the people to vote all of the time and all of the people who only vote some of the time, then who cares if all of the people don't vote all of the time?

That's crystal clear, isn't it?

7

Why Opinion Polls Don't Make Policy ... And It Ain't Cuz of Principle

A young congressman once said, "Public opinion polls don't affect how I think about issues, but they will affect how I talk about them."

He was really saying that public opinion had little to do with how he thought—or would vote. Good for him! He at least told the truth about what most politicos believe but rarely say.

Public opinion doesn't have a lot to do with how most legislators cast their votes. Surprised? No one should be who understands those who seek public office and those who support them. Most professional politicians, especially those who attain leadership positions, know jolly well what their own philosophical views are. They seek public office to implement specific ideas, not to sublimate them to any current public whim. They attain office because of financial support they receive from varied political single-issue interests who ascertain in advance the candidate's view on their favorite issues.

Political activists, especially the liberal Democrats, don't work to elect political weather vanes who can be swayed by passing public tempests. They strive hard for candidates who are supportive of their issues, who will "dance with the one's that brought'm to the ball" and who are emotionally equipped to tack around the strongest gale of public opinion. Sophisticated special interests look long and hard at the candidates before they contribute dollars, especially if those interests' financial well being is directly affected by the legislature.

The state and national capitols are loaded with lobbyists, most of whom either feed at the governmental trough or are taxed to pay for the chow. Unions as well as large corporations can lose or gain tens of millions of dollars by legislative policies established by incumbents. These large entities employ lobbyists to represent them, and they would be fools not to stay current on those in or those seeking public office.

Unfortunately, those almost totally under-represented are the small business community and the broad middle class. They cannot individually afford professional lobbyists. These good people ask little of government and wish only to be left alone. Obviously they're not.

Let me show you a conversation that will never take place. Imagine government employee union members talking to their union's political action committee (PAC) about which candidates their union PAC should financially support:

"How much money should we give to Charlie Goodguy?"

Member A: "Isn't he the candidate who wants to cut the size of the bureaucracy, especially our agency?"

"Yep, that's him."

Member B: "Isn't he running against Senator Southpaw, the man who voted for funding for all our departments?"

"Yep, that's right. However, Charlie Goodguy is fiscally correct when he says the taxpayer is overtaxed and our departments are getting too bureaucratic. For the good of the citizens, we must recognize the truth of what Mr. Goodguy says and cut back the number of state employees even if it includes our union membership. So, I recommend we max out, give heavily to Charlie Goodguy till it hurts. Why? Because it means GGS (Good Government Stuff)!"

Amidst huzzahs, hurrahs, and choruses of "He's a jolly good fella," the union votes unanimously for funding candidate Goodguy and cutting off contributions to Senator Southpaw.

How's that for wild fiction?

The day that trial lawyers lobby for quick and speedy trials, bureaucratic agencies demand financial cuts, and solons vote for returning to a part-time citizen legislature is the day Bambi is really the king of beasts and a Clinton is voted to replace George Washington on Mt. Rushmore.

The fact is, trial lawyers profit from long trials. Governmental employee unions look for and spend megabucks on candidates to continuously feather their nests. Once legislators are elected, do you think some public opinion poll will really impact their vote, thereby cutting campaign contributions and support from the very groups that got the politicians elected in the first place? Fat chance.

The only hot public opinion issues legislators really care about are those that can be organized by their opponents into fundraisers and converted into votes on election day. Most legislators, especially those who hold districts gerrymandered to their advantage, know that their opponents will not have enough juice to exploit their weaknesses. With incumbency, staff, and fundraising power, most officeholders know their opponents rarely can match them dollar for dollar in wooing the public. They also know that this year's hot issue is next year's cold memory. Only a small percentage of the population carry a beef against an incumbent over into the next year and, as I've said before, only if they are reminded, organized, registered, and turned out at election time.

This is a very important point.

Why then do good guys constantly fret over influencing public opinion? Why do businesses spend millions on advertising campaigns to create a better image for their corporations when attacked by some environmentalist group? Because most conservatives and businessmen don't know any better. They might know how to sell their products competitively, but the vast majority don't understand squat about political confrontation or how the leftists organize. Contrary to public perception, most businessmen operate on a much higher ethical level than those running attack ads against them.

Do you honestly believe most legislators really care what all the Joe Dokes think if those ideas can't be translated into power and implemented at election time? That takes organization.

Think about it. Public opinion can't put anyone in jail, take away property, or restrict anyone's behavior, unless it first becomes implemented through law.

Public opinion polls don't influence a politician's decision to introduce certain legislation unless it furthers what he wanted to do in the first place. More often than not, public opinion is manufactured to set the stage for leftist legislation. Politicians hold public hearings, form investigative committees, call in their left-wing professors to testify, send out reams of press releases, schedule talk shows, have favorable editorials in the *Washington Post* and get as many media interviews as possible. Then, after enough generated hoopla and boola boola, Senator Southpaw introduces a bill based on a recent poll taken by The Portside Institute. Sound familiar?

If public opinion really meant anything, we would have speedy trials and executions of repeat rapists, murderers, and child kidnappers, and we'd be saddled with little national debt. Needless to say, we'd also have real welfare reform, curtailed illegal immigration, and a balanced budget.

On rare occasions, an issue can be so hot and organized that the leftist legislators will dialectically cast a vote contrary to their actual wishes. Then, when the heat dies down, the politicos will find multiple ways to legislatively circumvent their prior votes.

The death penalty is a good example. Although the death penalty became law, the humanist politicians have done much to delay actual executions. A proliferation of endless appeals, gubernatorial pardons, admissions of "new" evidence, and stays by left-wing appointed judges is the norm.

On high-intensity public issues, leftists will introduce good-sounding but ineffective legislation. By controlling the bill, they can steer the direction the issue takes. After lengthy hearings, teams of witnesses, reams of research, and pounds of pontification, the weak legislation—if public fervor has subsided enough—is quietly killed. It can, of course, become weak law, then ineffectively enforced.

An irritated public often stages rallies, marches, and demonstrations to voice its ire in hopes that such demonstrations will affect public opinion and thus influence the legislature. In reality, they have little impact on the legislators. They are effective only if they are part of a permanent, organized, long-range program to change the leftist-controlled legislature. Such demonstrations may occasionally appear to make an impression, but a short time later the leftists revert to their old ways. Things will soon be back the way they were.

Affecting public opinion has its place if it is used to organize for a specific goal. On most issues, legislators know that public opinion is shallow and temporary, changing in intensity as a new issue arises. *What the majority of people think in January hasn't much to do with election results in November, and that is the most important thing to remember.*

A number of years ago in California, the gun-grabbing left beat the drums for crime control through gun control. They introduced a ballot initiative calling for handgun confiscation. The media picked up the beat and after awhile—guess what? Polls showed the initiative had a two-to-one favorable public opinion. When the election was held, due to the effective work of the pro-gun forces, the public got a good whiff of what the proposed law would do ... and the initiative lost two to one. Was the first poll wrong? Probably not. Polling is much like taking a photo of a horse race at the quarter pole. It accurately tells you who's leading but can't tell you who the eventual winner will be.

Polling can be extremely valuable and accurate; it is an excellent tool when used properly to analyze issues for elective purposes. It can be one of the most powerful weapons in our conservative arsenal. But, does it really affect what legislators do or think? Not really, especially if it can't be converted into votes at election time.

8

Move That Fulcrum
and Start Making a Difference Today

It has been said that if one moved the fulcrum far enough, the weight of a single man could leverage the world.

Politics is the art of leverage, knowing how to move the fulcrum. How? By comprehending that a minority of people can control the direction of government by controlling a minority of the voters. Elected office is a leveraged position with politicians having police power and the ability to control the purse strings.

Gaining control of the legislature is a massive leverage. Understanding how to influence those who are elected is leverage. A key part of this knowledge is knowing in which districts one should expend energy and money and in which districts it is a waste of time.

As explained in the chapter on the percentages of politics, registering new voters around specific issues and turning them out on primary election day is an example of moving the fulcrum.

Many decent people waste an inordinate amount of time angrily coping with, and battling, some agency of government. Fighting bureaucracy is like pummeling a large balloon. One can sink one's arm into the balloon up to the shoulder and then watch it puff back to its original shape once the fist is removed. No matter how hard you punch and no matter how long you keep it up, once you stop striking it resumes its original shape and seems to grow larger. Exhaustion—financial, mental, and physical—is the usual reward for directly fighting a large bureaucracy. A citizen's feeble effort doesn't seem to bother the bureaucrats a whit. Why should it?

Those who run bureaucracies are used to complaints. They look upon the balloon beaters as bothersome malcontents, nothing more than momentary glitches that must be tolerated as part of the job. They know that time is on their side. There's no down side for them, no financial pain, no loss of work, and no lawyer to hire to protect their personal interests. They can have counsel at taxpayers' expense. At their fingertips are entire departments filled with bureaucratic barristers and public relations personnel. In many instances, they also have administrative law on their side. Often the appeals process requires the complainant to go through a lengthy administrative process before he can ever get to the courts. In other words, the deck is stacked in favor of the agency and against the citizen.

Why should we expect anything else? Is anyone naïve enough to think that once an agency swells and becomes a large bureaucracy that it remains a servant of the people and not primarily an agent for its own self-interest?

In spite of the obvious no-win results which are preordained by the nature of the conflict, good guys continue to assault the governmental agencies with hopes of victory and receiving, at best, just momentary relief.

Am I saying there is no way to win when fighting the bureaucracy directly? Pretty much. The chance of winning a direct confrontation is marginal at best. The battlefield is strewn with the bodies of unsuccessful citizens who thought they could win in a direct battle with the bureaucrats; inevitably, they were gummed to death in the yawing mouth of bureaucracy.

There is a way to attack that does yield results. But it does not consist of punching yourself out, flailing away at the bulbous bureaucratic mass. Every balloon has a valve where the air seeps in and out. For the bureaucracy, the air is money. The valve that controls the money flow is the legislature. Elected officials fill the balloon, and they are the ones who can deflate it as well. I have yet to meet a bureaucrat who will work for love alone; they all like payday. Bureaucrats may kiss-off complaints, but they kiss-up to elected officials.

Should one ever tackle the bureaucracy? Sometimes—if the fight against the agency can be used to rally angry, gored citizens around political action, where funds can be raised and animosity leveraged into sophisticated political action at election time.

Once the legislators see an agency as a liability, they have the ability to curtail it or eliminate the agency in its entirety. Remember, he who has the gold rules—especially in politics. The legislature controls the purse strings, and every bureaucrat knows it. Why waste time, money, and energy fighting "the government" (bureaucrats) when the same effort could have a direct impact on those who control the valve? That's leverage. Public employee unions have political action committees that contribute to candidates; I can't think of one that does not. They know where the valve is located and who dumps in the dollars.

We need to learn to be patient, know what we are doing and target our energies without wasting time on fruitless endeavors. Conservatives should be in the business of controlling the fulcrum and by applying pressure, leveraging far greater numbers.

Imagine a teeter-totter with a three-hundred-pound bureaucrat on one end and you on the other. To control the scale, one needs to be three hundred and one pounds or more to tilt the teeter-totter.

As explained earlier, only a small percentage of the citizenry casts primary ballots, thereby deciding for others, the non-voters, what their political future will be. The persistent voter has some leverage; his or her one ballot decides for as many as five non-voters.

When one factors in the world population of billions, the American voter has no idea how powerful his vote happens to be. Without question, the United States is recognized as the most powerful nation in the world; our elected officials therefore lead and, in some cases, direct world policy. One American primary voter leverages worldwide the destiny of one hundred others. One's vote doesn't count? You bet it does! That's actually an awesome responsibility when you think about it.

It stands to reason that those who control blocs of votes and campaign money have even greater leverage. Being a part of an active, sophisticated PAC or similar politically organized group has great impact.

Once elected, a city councilman decides the spending of millions of tax dollars, a state representative votes on the expenditure of billions, and a congressman trillions. That's leverage. Once in leadership, the officeholder can establish who gets what, who works for government and who doesn't. That's power—awesome leverage.

Having the attention of an elected official is leverage. Writing a single letter to him has marginal effect, unless it is part of an organized campaign. Writing to him as a leader of an effective political action committee or politically organized group is leverage. If your group is large enough or mean enough, this is the most powerful leverage of all.

Of course, communicating to him as a valuable member of his campaign finance committee is get-your-phone-calls-answered-immediately leverage. Keep in mind that a five-hundred-dollar contribution to a candidate in a hotly contested primary is big bucks. If given directly to the candidate, he'll clearly remember who gave it. However, five hundred dollars to an incumbent in a large district is chicken feed—usually expected, often taken for granted and, at best, vaguely remembered.

Knowing when to apply leverage is also leverage.

Politics is a world where perceptions become the reality. Obviously, the desired effect is to be perceived as an eight-hundred-pound political gorilla. If you achieve that image, you'll be surprised how many people will bring you nice yellow bananas. Numerical size is important but not imperative. Which breed of a dog would cause apprehension and fear: a lovable playful two-hundred-pound tail-wagging mutt or a snarling thirty-five-pound pit-bull that's known to bite? Size isn't everything; leverage is.

Choosing which organizations to support is also leverage for you. Who, as the expression goes, gives you the best bang for the buck? A number of conservative organizations are sizeable, but do they affect politics? Do they spin off PAC groups? Are they directly affecting large blocs of votes? Do they organize and take action in and around elections? Are they mean and tough, or do they just throw money at incumbents? Do they constantly send out depressing literature, pointing out some new inequity but offering little political direction on what to do about it? If they're not effective with their dollars, participating in primaries, and electing good guys or harming bad guys, then think long and hard about the next dollar you send them.

People are surprised, sometimes shocked, by the answer I give when asked about my preference for president. I usually answer, "I don't pay much attention to who's running for that office."

If pressed for details as to why I don't pay much attention to the number one office, I tell them I personally don't have much influence over what the president does, so it's fruitless to waste my time fussing about who he may be. Presidents don't return my phone calls or seek my advice. However, local officials, state legislators, congressmen, a number of U.S. senators and a few gubernatorial aspirants do. They have an interest in me because I can, and often do, have some impact on their elections through my writings, the PACs and other political groups I have formed, and other political organizations I influence. Why waste time thinking about politicians who won't care what I say or do when I can deal with candidates and officeholders who do?

Why do conservatives waste their breath discussing politicians beyond their influence when there are officeholders they can directly impact? The answers are varied. But a significant reason is that there is little personal pain when discussing presidential politics, especially if your man loses. On the other hand, when a local candidate you supported goes down in defeat, you can be held personally responsible. Waxing eloquently about national presidential elections is esoteric and blue sky; personal involvement in local and state elections truly proves one's commitment to good government.

Politics is like baseball. Few make it to the big leagues unless they first learn their skills in the minors. First, get involved at the local level, then state, and then, if you have learned the trade, you may play in the big leagues. Most conservatives have been fans, sitting in the bleachers, leaving the field of play to the left.

It is most ironic. Those who hate big government and purportedly advocate local control don't participate at the level where they can have the most immediate impact. The leftists, knowing that local offices serve as the starting point—the farm system to higher positions—seek out and fill seats on school boards, city councils, and the myriad of commissions and districts. A local office is an excellent place to build a base of operations. The citizenry, although they complain about politics, choose more readily from those with experience in politics.

I can't tell you how many conservatives I have interviewed who are willing to serve in government—starting at the top. The fact that they have cursory knowledge of the methodology of politics doesn't seem to bother them at all, even after they lose. Americans may be ignorant, but they aren't fools. They prefer someone with a modicum of know-how. The one with no experience whatsoever rarely wins.

Working in local elections is spring training in the minor leagues. Virtually all the big-name stars start there. Control the bottom, and one day you control the top. One day the man you elected to city council becomes the state senator and then moves to Congress and talks to the president on your behalf. If you really become effective, one day the phone rings and you are asked to come to Washington to advise the president. Somebody is leveraging the president at this very moment. Why not you?

9

Press the Hot Buttons
to Get Good Things Going

We have a very valuable tool if we learn how to use it. It's called punching the hot button—practically everyone has one.

Those conservatives who know where to punch and organize to do so are successful in beating up the left. They pick up victories in the process, sometimes winning contrary to mass public opinion.

The hot button varies from one individual to another. It can be any issue that causes deep emotion and righteous indignation. It may be excessive taxation, regulation, abortion, gun rights, euthanasia, crime, environment, unions—you name it. Just about everyone, even the most politically lethargic, can be aroused if his or her hot button is pushed.

There is a decided difference between how humanists perceive hot button issues and how we do. Hard-leftists, knowingly or unknowingly, operate on the false assumption that class warfare exists. They erroneously believe that segments of our population are constantly in conflict with one another—each segment battling over power. Thus, the road to humanist power is to politicize these different classes. The concept is pure Marx, although many leftists haven't a glimmer of who originated the concept.

Most liberals, like bit actors in a play, haven't an inkling of whose idea they are emoting; they accept it and act it out. Karl Marx taught that natural animosity exists between segments of society—men against women, labor against management, blacks against whites, rich against poor, young against old—each with their own logic. Like most effective lies, it has some element of truth to it. There are some basic differences between people. However, not to the degree where we are segregated into classes by race, wealth, or occupation, each with opposing, antagonistic thoughts and interests. Remember, to the left, there is no common reasoning that binds us all together, rules that govern all our behavior, nor immutable laws applicable to all and written in each heart.

Rejecting God's laws and following their own set of assumptions, the liberals often approach voters solely as members of a class. The elderly, minorities, labor, and women are expected to support the left's candidates because they are pro-labor, pro-elderly, pro-woman, etc. This idea is derived from the assumption that we are nothing more than matter in motion, evolutionary beasts, controlled by our environment, advanced animals whose thoughts are influenced totally by our class. *In the absence of any other approach, it works.*

I say it again, in the absence of any other approach . . . . To appeal to each class, the left must by necessity use propaganda to appeal to that class. The leftist rifle shoots to a segment of the population, appealing to one group at a time around class concepts.

The census bureau, following class-concept jargon, categorizes voters by age, employment, income, race, occupation, and nation of origin, etc. They then make this data available. In the language of political junkies, it's called demographic information. The leftists use this information effectively when campaigning, sending specific information geared to the identified class. In absence of any other technique, Marxist class warfare works more often than it fails.

Class then, to a leftist, is of prime importance. Issues are of secondary importance.

Is there a better way?

You bet there is!

Marx's class warfare concept relegates people to a caste system of thought where age, occupation, race, and gender are the dominant motivations. Although such characterizations have some influence, they aren't the driving forces behind an individual's behavior.

People, given a diversification of talents by God, are issue-oriented. Some subjects are so boiling hot and incendiary that they overpower and out-motivate any class differences that may exist. Issues such as abortion blast across race, ethnic, and economic lines with passionate intensity. Others, such as the Second Amendment, right to work, family values, and excessive taxation, take mild-mannered, gentle citizens and transform them into placard-carrying zealots.

People are creative, spiritual, possessing great ingenuity, and capable of elevating mankind to great heights, far outstripping any temporal circumstances in which they may find themselves. We have been given the power to do so by our Creator; we have been given dominion, reason, and purpose to life. Ideas, concepts, and values are the juice that moves men and women. It makes little difference what our age, sex, social rank, or color happens to be; controversial issues drive people into passionate action.

Restrictive gun laws are a perfect example. This subject cuts across all social lines and obliterates party registration, color, and ethnic considerations. It is a fiery hot-button subject to a segment of the American population. Pun intended, the right to own firearms is a high-powered, high-velocity issue that targets many a heart, mine included.

Everyone with an IQ over 50 has a hot button—everyone. The list of such points of contention is growing, not shrinking. The socialist programs haven't worked, and every day somebody new is gored by regulation, taxation, and moral corruption in high places. We should rejoice, leap with joy, when socialist programs fail. Our country is in a mess because bad programs have bad effects. Why should that make us gloomy? Think how depressing it would be if socialism worked.

Again, issues drive people. Our job is to identify people one by one, educate them around their hot buttons, register them to vote, organize them, and turn them out for political action and on Election Day.

Let's review how the typical conservative candidate, Mr. Wright, sends out literature to the voters. The standard procedure is to put together a brochure relating how he honestly feels on most issues, then send it to every voter in the district. In the campaign piece, Mr. Wright identifies ten subjects dear to his heart.

The brochure is received by Mr. Gump, a man who usually votes. Mr. Gump agrees with Mr. Wright on most of the issues, such as the right to own guns, excessive taxes, and family values but one of the points gores his ox. Mr. Gump is a factory worker and his union has often told him that the right to work issue would cost him his job.

The leftist candidate, Mr. Wrong, sends Gump a slick pamphlet telling him that he, Mr. Wrong, is not only endorsed by Gump's union, but he loves motherhood, blue sky, and little else. Mr. Wrong doesn't explain that he's for gun confiscation, expansion of government, thinks abortion is just a "choice," and that he has been endorsed by and has received contributions from all the homosexual clubs in San Francisco and Hollywood.

The day before the election, the union calls Mr. Gump, tells him to vote Wrong and that Wright is too far to the right. Guess how Mr. Gump will vote?

What would the outcome have been if Mr. Gump had been identified beforehand as being good on the issues of family, guns, and taxes, and had then been told by a pro-family group that candidate Wrong was endorsed by the "National Association of Lesbians and Gays"? What if the organizations favoring candidate Wright had only communicated to Mr. Gump on those predetermined areas of common interest? Would it make a difference? I believe there's little doubt about it. Americans aren't dumb, just uninformed on many facts important to them.

Another important point. In the closing moments of campaigns, literature received directly from candidates is usually looked upon as self-serving propaganda, especially if the material is derogatory of the opposition.

The same negative material coming from an independent organization is more believable. A pro-gun group telling a pro-gun voter that office-seeker Mr. Wrong is bad on guns, is far more believable than the same information coming from his opponent.

In the past, the task of predetermining how each voter feels on issues would have been extremely difficult. But with the advent of PCs (personal computers), it is not only possible, it is becoming more cost effective to do so. Printing a brochure detailing the candidate's platform and mailing it to every voter only works if the opponent is equally naive. The candidate who identifies the hot buttons of individuals in his constituency, registers them, effectively communicates, and turns enough of them out to the polls will usually win no matter what the registration disadvantages.

If the leftists continue to pander to class concepts while we identify the hot-button voters and get them out on Election Day, then chances of our victory improve immeasurably, even against incumbents. The left is operating mainly on a flawed concept that inhibits them. Their bad ideas work to our advantage. *But*, we succeed only if we capitalize on their errors and exploit their mistakes.

Working in a phone bank, calling potential voters in order to identify hot buttons (HB), registering them, door-to-door contact, holding a backyard fundraiser or coffee hour for a good-guy candidate pays great dividends. Learn how the game is played, then excel in it.

Tens of millions of citizens aren't registered to vote. If we approach them via their HB, they can be rallied around a decent candidate. With so few voters turning out in the primaries and multiple candidates running for office, the leverage factor is enormous if we prioritize our efforts.

Scripture speaks quite clearly about how God created each of us with different talents, different interests; each individual unique, each held accountable for the talents given and capable of differentiating between right and wrong. Nowhere does Scripture mention class-consciousness or multiple forms of contrary logic. There is but one logic, one morality—God's. Let's take advantage of how the Almighty has made us and appeal to the less politically motivated around the issues that set their minds afire.

This requires us to search for the hot button, not argue at the drop of a hat and chase away those who don't have an interest in all facets of politics. Patience is a blessing, and as long as we strive and persevere, believe me, time is on our side. The old expression, "You can lead a horse to water but you can't make him drink" is true. But stand around the trough long enough, and sooner or later, he'll take a sip.

We traditional Americans who grasp the abstracts of confrontational politics must assume leadership and see ourselves as the vanguard in the restructuring and reconstituting of a constitutional America as envisioned by our forefathers.

Leadership emerges from the ones who properly understand the nature of the struggle, learn what works in politics, and act upon that knowledge. The solution is always found in understanding the problem and then acting organizationally with others. *Knowledge is power—but only when it is translated into behavior.*

10

Perseverance and Professionalism

The humanists built their control of America incrementally, bits at a time, by a series of both small- and medium-sized conflicts; winning some, losing others, but with each, building residuals, gaining recruits, propagandizing, putting structure together and learning from each confrontation. Even when one of their issues is defeated, no net loss occurs if a residual is gained, especially when new activists are gained and trained. They are constantly on the attack, never defending, always invading and gaining some ground while expanding influence along the way.

In every confrontation, the left has little to lose since their opposition rarely attacks or takes advantage of organizational opportunities. Most traditionalists are content with protecting the status quo, compromising and going back to sleep. Only occasionally do leftists have to defend their own territory or the legislation they have already implemented. Once begun, like a malignant growth, the social programs become a part of the system, often named an "entitlement" and deemed untouchable.

The record of the Republican-controlled Congress from 1994–2006 amply proves this point, especially when one considers how the leftist agenda was advanced even during the years Republicans controlled both the Congress and the White House (2001–2006).

The reason is that every new leftist agenda is intended to create an area of influence, to develop a new corps of followers with a vested interest in maintaining and expanding the new program. Conversely, their traditionalist opposition rarely thinks in long-term goals or of developing residuals from any engagement. Up until recently, building a constituency for a protracted fight wasn't even considered by conservatives. They thought of themselves only as defenders of the status quo.

The left builds and trains professionals in the art of confrontational politics, each conflict viewed as having long-range benefits. Due to the ignorance and poor methodology of their opposition, the left has, so far, little downside risk.

The humanist leaders are not giddy, well-meaning amateurs giving their time only on weekends. They realize that it takes professionalism to move their agenda constantly and affect the legislative process. Advancement cannot be sustained for any length of time by voluntary help. Over the years, the liberals have developed a cadre of skilled, full-time employees to guide, implement, and propagandize their causes. They have been systematically placed in foundations, governmental agencies, union leadership, college faculties, and staffs of leftist organizations and legislators. On the other side, the conservative opposition occasionally puts forth a valiant effort, hoping volunteerism will suffice but often losing because they usually show up too late with too little. By the time they get organized, the fight is usually over, and they disband.

Before the good guys can consistently win, we too must professionalize to take advantage of the mess leftist programs create. This professionalization in no way minimizes the need for volunteer hard work. But when an organization gets large enough to have a consistent, year-by-year impact, it is extremely difficult to accomplish the day-by-day activities of money raising, lobbying, letter writing, phoning, etc., with only volunteers. Just when you need volunteers the most, something will come up to deter their efforts, such as family issues, employment, vacations, etc.

It is sometimes easier to raise money and hire someone—full-time if possible—than to deal constantly with volunteer help. A myriad of details always develops with any major effort, and something will invariably disappear through the cracks when part-time help is involved.

This is not to imply that one must professionalize before starting a project. Many a successful activity begins as a volunteer effort. But over the long conflict ahead of us, professionalization must be a goal. We are not fighting hare-brained ideological amateurs or giddy social misfits. We are fighting professionals, and we will never beat them as idealistic, well-intentioned, sometimes starry-eyed, once-in-a-while participants.

We are in a life-long, protracted conflict with those who do evil. Part-time effort won't cut the mustard. If one doesn't have the time, then at the very least, become a financially supporting member of existing professional conservative organizations. A growing number of them already out there cover a wide range of single-issue interests. If none of them suits your fancy, then organize one that can do a better job. But don't just sit on the sidelines and complain about those who are trying. To put it bluntly, we organize, then professionalize or watch the American dream die. The good guys who think politically are a small minority, but so what? We always have been, and we always will be. But—so are the leftists.

Politically, which one of us organizes the best, using the material and issues presented to us?

Sophisticated political action begins long before the general public gets an inkling of what will happen in the next election. Potential candidates are often selected and evaluated many months, even years, before they run for office. Only those who pay daily attention to the legislative process know who might retire, where the new district lines will be drawn, where shifts in population are occurring, changes in district registration, who offers good political management, and who the hacks are. Politics is filled with the latter and has few of the former.

Incompetent and inadequate management can stay in business year after year because of the influx of new, wet-behind-the-ear candidates. It takes capable, experienced professionals to know which is which; they watch all of the nuances of the elective process. It really requires full-time attention to keep up with all of the political shifting, especially in large states and at the national level.

Amateurs rarely succeed in electing anyone for the higher offices. *Mr. Smith Goes to Washington* makes for a good movie, happy tears, and spilled popcorn, but that's about all. And besides, in the movie, Mr. Smith was appointed, not elected.

American traditionalists will run government when they organize. There is nothing to stop conservatives from building strength around issues, establishing structure, giving leadership on key popular subjects, having their own professional lobbyists, networking with other structures, cooperating with them in the selection of primary candidates, and then winning in the General Election.

The rank and file of pro-life, pro-gun, home schoolers, taxpayer lobbies, right-to-work, and pro-defense groups may not realize what they have in common. They usually all have the same political opposition, whether they know it or not. As long as each organization's leadership understands the need to network with the other conservative groups, that is what really matters.

No battle should be engaged without considering long-range goals and the residual benefits gained. We must constantly ask if we can leverage this fight to our advantage. Besides potential victory, what other benefits will accrue? Will we emerge with additional workers to fight the next battle? Will we have a bank of volunteer names, donor lists, and trained leadership? Did we fight on their territory or were we just defending our own? Did we reframe the issue, build for the future? Did we divert their leftist designs and profit from their mistakes? Will the left look upon this as a loss, or did they gain any ground at our expense? Was the fight really worth the effort or should we have used our energy and money elsewhere? Did we emerge from the confrontation depressed or elated? Are our forces ready for the next engagement? These questions and more must be answered with brutal objectivity.

We can learn from our enemies' methodology without having to adopt any of their fallacious premises or underhanded tactics.

They look for weaknesses and then exploit them; so can we. Telling the truth about our opponent's weakness is no crime.

They build residuals; so can we.

They think in terms of victory; so can we.

They understand leverage; so can we.

We must never forget that the radical humanists have had to overcome immense obstacles to get where they are now. They have massaged atheistic concepts into the body politic of a nation of believers. That wasn't an easy task. Our job is to organize and recapture the American dream. This shouldn't be too hard; that is, if we persevere. We have the time. The clock is on our side—as long as we keep winding it up.

11

Making Lemonade with Rough Hands

We must learn to peek behind the verbal glitz and glitter that covers any new humanist cause. Why? In order to discover what they're really promoting and be able to take advantage of it. Often, what they say isn't what they mean nor is it what they are attempting to do. Look hard enough and long enough and the true hypocrisy shows through. Inevitably, it's a grab for more power and can, incidentally, be an opportunity for us. You can bet, whatever they're up to, somebody's ox will be gored.

As an example, several years ago, the radical environmentalists announced the spotted owl was an endangered species. They immediately took the high ground shouting, "Save the owl!" They centered the entire debate around the owls' potential extinction and placed the blame on those greedy lumbermen who preferred wealth to the future of this rare and jeopardized bird. The lumber industry reacted like most confused, non-confrontational businessmen do. It accepted the false premise, allowing the whole dispute to be focused on the owl being endangered, thereby preordaining their eventual defeat. They were trapped, framed, snookered into a "when-did-you-stop-beating-your-owl" issue.

If the environmental clan were really interested in spotted owls and if the eco-nuts were as numerous as they said they were, they could have all chipped-in, set up a foundation, purchased some forests and protected the feathered fowl to their heart's content.

They didn't attempt to buy one acre.

They demanded that those who owned the valuable timberland set aside vast tracts of harvestable forest. As usual, they advanced their causes with other people's dimes, not theirs. The radical left saw a ripe opportunity for political growth in their environmental numbers in government by jumping on this particular "cause." As usual, following on the heels of the attack, legislation was introduced. Substantial sympathy amongst leftist legislators already existed for the introduction of such bills. All that was needed was a populist reason.

Angering the lumber industry and placing many jobs in jeopardy did not bother the tree huggers in the least. The spotted owl gave them another reason for the expansion of their cause and for regulatory control over another major industry. Owl protection is as good a cause as any.

Facts now show the bird was never in jeopardy, but at the time, the little hooters were reported to be down to their last hoot. As long as the timber people argued whether or not the owl was endangered, the industry was destined to lose. The left knows that factual data often fails when pitted against organized deceit. Whether the owl was endangered or not was never the real question or the real concern. It was just another good reason to expand the power of the environmental cause, a real win-win situation for them.

Would the environmentalists-humanists pursue the saving of the owl if they thought it would diminish their overall power in Congress? Of course not! They judged correctly that their strength would increase through the confrontation and that new recruits would be gathered around this "motherhood owl" debate. The left properly surmised the lumber industry would respond like Pavlov's dog. By reacting on cue, the entire industry clumsily played right into the environmentalist's hands.

What could the lumber industry have done differently? Plenty!

When handed a lemon, make lemonade. Had the industry immediately understood the political implications, it could have punished the humanist cause substantially by organizing all the affected parties into political action committees (PACs), raising substantial dollars and targeting vulnerable incumbents for defeat. The industries affected were enormous—housing, furniture, foresters, their unions, suppliers, construction companies. The list of users of wood products is long indeed. They needed to give only cursory attention to the owl issue and could have dismissed it as a silly guise for the creation of more government jobs. But they bit on the bait and believing it was a public concern, they credited the radical liberals with sincere altruistic motives of "saving the owl." Even if this were true and the public was interested (which it wasn't), so what? As stated before, public opinion over an issue like this has but nominal impact on how a legislator votes.

The lumber industry should have calmly and forcibly shown members of Congress that megabucks were ready to go after those bold enough to vote against them. Had congressional leadership known that their environmental allies were creating an implacable, well-financed and politically astute enemy, would the owl have been given a hoot on Capitol Hill? I doubt it.

I asked some members of the lumber community the following questions. "Do you believe the Democrat congressional leadership would have paid much attention to the owl issue if they knew millions of dollars would be effectively used against vulnerable Democrat incumbents?" Obviously, no. "Would the Congress of thirty years ago have even considered legislation with such specious facts put forth as evidence?" Again, an obvious no.

It takes leftist Democrat legislators and confrontationally inadequate Republicans to pass socialist programs. The way to defeat the humanists is to take advantage of their causes—organize effective opposition, professionalize staff, build a war chest of funds, target weak incumbents, joyfully punish the adversaries, and stay in the fight until the last liberal is retired from office and you accomplish your goals.

Remember, when the left encounters effective opposition, they will dialectically step back in order to consolidate gains and, at that moment, offer compromise. *When we accept compromise at this point, in order to cease the hostilities, it is a serious mistake! This is a time of great opportunity!*

The leftist retreat shows that the opposition is formidable and should be aggressively continued. The left will, because of their methodology, take one step backward, expecting the pressure to subside. But if it persists, *they will retreat even further!* If the aggressive attack continues, they will panic and get personally vicious—a sure sign they are losing. Why? Because beneath the thin, hard leftist veneer, they're nasty people. Rub it off, and you'll see soon enough.

Humanists are totally unaccustomed to a defensive posture. It is not compatible with their past experiences, and they are not used to it. And certainly, they are not expecting or prepared for it. They have for so many years perceived their opposition as soft, simplistic buffoons, religious simpletons, adhering to ideas that are antiquated, bankrupt, and no longer relevant. They see us as incapable of stopping their sophisticated, intelligent advance. Therefore, they do not give any meaningful credit to us. They attribute our civility as weakness and deem our opposition to their proposals as desperate and useless gyrations of a dying culture. They expect no real, persistent resistance, so they are extremely vulnerable and totally unprepared whenever an effective counterattack occurs. They are completely surprised when we leverage off of their efforts, form effective political and campaign operations and whip them in the political arena.

If, for example, the lumbermen had gathered together those many businesses negatively affected by the owl issue, organized them politically, networked with other conservative groups and brought about the defeat of several marginal congressmen, the message would have been loud and clear. Congress would have quickly deduced that supporting the environmental owl issue equals net loss.

We must learn to build alliances and collect residuals in any and all confrontations with the left. Even when temporarily set back by election losses, organizations can be held together for the next encounter, a fight which will inevitably take place. From each conflict something can and must be gained—experience, friendships, political skills, fundraising files, evaluation of talent, and the building of potential candidates. The continual building of ongoing structure is vitally important. Good candidates and future skills come from fighting in the trenches and participating in campaigns. A farm system develops out of political conflict where new talent is trained by the rough hands of trial and error.

It is abundantly clear that those who are elected to public office with no prior experience with confrontation will be easily intimidated, chewed up by the other side, and completely ineffective when put in daily contact with trained leftists. Usually, candidates who run for office with only business experience are the most naïve and vulnerable. Business experience alone prepares no one for political office. I've seen many a successful businessman wilt under the pressure of political confrontation.

When a new humanist program surfaces, look upon it as just another lemon. Grab it, squeeze the "L" out of 'em, and make lemonade.

12

"Learn Good" to Turn On Your Brain, Before Turning on Your Mouth

Jesse Unruh, the liberal
Democrat leader of the California state assembly during the
Reagan gubernatorial years, once said, "I don't learn fast, but I
learn good!" Maybe Jesse wasn't grammatically correct, but he
did, indeed, "learn good." Nobody politically bent California to
the port side more dramatically than "Big Daddy Unruh." It is
obvious we conservatives are also slow learners; maybe it's time
we "learned good" as well. Maybe it's true that our heads are as
hard as our principles.

Another old political codger once admonished me for trying
to "educate" the voter during an election. I thought he was
wrong, dead wrong. I was a slow learner regarding that fact.
After clumsily stumbling through several election cycles, I found
out he was right.

I finally decided to relate to what the public knows, not what
I thought they should know. I learned the hard way that trying to
"better educate" the voters on complex issues lost more votes
than it gained.

It's not that we can't and shouldn't educate, but there is a
time and place for everything. It's the "when" that's important.
Instruction should take place after the election, not while running for office. Theodore Roosevelt called elective office "a
bully pulpit." He was absolutely right. An officeholder has a
wide and often attentive audience; that is, if he is wise and

industrious enough to know when to take advantage of his opportunities to educate.

During the closing months of an election campaign, the general voters' attention span is short, and they rarely take the time or effort to deeply contemplate controversial, complex issues. When local crime is their chief concern, they're not too interested in a dissertation on the supposed evils of the Federal Reserve System. They are interested in how the candidate thinks about what affects them now. *They want to know how the candidate feels about* their *favorite hot button issue, not his.*

Time, bias, money, and human nature work against the education of the citizenry, especially at election time, when doubt and cynicism cause voters to question most candidates' truthfulness. The voting public is a mixed bag of knowledge, prejudice, false assumptions, and wisdom. It is much better when a candidate can ascertain where the voters' interests lie and find out what punches their hot buttons.

This is where polling becomes a very vital part of a campaign. Another wise old political duffer wisecracked, "If ya' want to discover the general popularity of sauerkraut, ya' don't ask folks at a German picnic." Too often that's what conservative candidates usually do. They attend conservative functions and talk to their friends to ascertain what issues are important to the general population. Dumb birds of a feather flunk together.

A good pollster can tell you voters' intensity on given issues. Successful politicians use survey data quite effectively. The rub comes when polling information shows the hot issue is XYZ and the candidate believes ABC. So, what do some office seekers do? For public perception and consumption, a political opportunist becomes an XYZ advocate until elected, then he votes ABC to his heart's content. Anyone whose ethics are situational has no trouble doing exactly that. For him, the objective is getting elected. The truth, during the heat of a campaign, is often irrelevant—sadly even to some conservatives.

Moral candidates don't lie; they find it reprehensible even to twist the truth. Contrary to opinion, there is no need for one to obfuscate facts or prevaricate in order to win. There are plenty of ways in which a moral candidate can campaign without abandoning principles. Sometimes, though, your favorite subject might have to take a back seat while the campaign zeros in on an issue much closer to the public's heart.

A good example is Gun Owners of California.

The Second Amendment issue is very important to our membership, and we are very desirous of electing pro-gun men and women. We learn in advance if a person is solid on our issue, before we endorse and financially support the candidate. However, we don't demand that the gun issue be the primary subject they campaign about. We know by experience and sophisticated polling that not all areas of California are pro-gun. We have a better chance of draining the Pacific Ocean than electing a pro-gun candidate in the city of San Francisco.

In some other urban areas, the general public is so monumentally misinformed on the gun issue that if a candidate made ownership of assault weapons his primary issue his chance of winning would be zero to none. When asked, we expect our candidate to frame the gun issue in the best light, relate to the audience by talking about protection of family, home, and the wide use of sporting firearms. When garnering votes and given a minute to speak, a candidate's attempt to educate a Hollywood Hills women's group about the more complex differences between a semi-auto military look-alike and a fully automatic UZI can turn into a net loss.

We certainly do not insist our candidates include ownership of AR-15s and AK-47s in their brochures. We look for and then help qualified candidates who show political astuteness, such as sophisticated campaign management and the ability to use survey data wisely.

Gun Owners of California has helped elect literally hundreds of candidates since our founding in 1975. *Never has one of them been elected on the gun issue. Gun money, yes, but not the gun issue.*

One of our best pro-gunner friends was a southern California state senator who won election on the issue of yellow streetlights. His opponent was a former mayor who took out the old white lights and installed yellow ones that the local populace hated. Fortunately, our man liked pretty white bulbs and, as the polling data and election confirmed, so did the voters.

Our membership has been delighted with the results of our judgment. In an extremely liberal environment and with a small percentage of the population, we've often held our own.

To many, GOP in California stands for Gun Owners Party. *I firmly believe that the sophistication of a political action committee can be judged by how many they elect around issues other than their own.*

My first election hinged upon the issue of property taxes and bureaucratic government. The subject of guns rarely came up. However, it was well known to the activist conservatives and to the pro-gunners in the district how I stood on key issues. Both were the core of my campaign team.

I didn't lie to anybody on an issue. But I was selective on what was placed in my campaign brochures and how I framed each subject. Once in office, I used the senate seat as a bully pulpit on a variety of conservative issues. My newspaper columns were carried statewide and in national publications. Fifty-six stations broadcast my weekly radio show. I regularly appeared on radio talk shows and TV advocating the citizen's Second Amendment rights. All these platforms would never have been possible for me if I hadn't first won the senate seat.

I am not advocating the giving up of principles. But I do think it wise to analyze the audience and to turn on the brain before one turns on the mouth.

13

Stop Educating and Start Organizing Around Hot Buttons

A number of years ago, I was waxing eloquently to an elderly acquaintance about how to pay off our national debt. After listening to my enlightened dissertation, the wise old gentleman threw me a book of wooden matches and said, "Here's some wood, build me a house."

I didn't understand so I dumbly asked, "What do you mean by that?"

He then explained to me that although the matchbox contained the wood ingredients, there wasn't enough of it to build anything, much less a home. He told me my esoteric "solution" required a complete change in the voting habits held by the majority of Congress. While others might share my illustrious ideas, few of them were elected to office. I had no real, practical plan, just a lot of hot ideas and wild hopes. Unless I could put the wood to my "solution"—including a way to elect a new Congress—my idea was just so much verbal smoke.

He was right. My solution to the national debt problem required a new majority in Congress with legislators committed to cutting the federal budget to the bone. I was expounding esoteric answers when the votes weren't there to make change occur. I had a goal but no road map, no vehicle, no methodology to get there.

Just about everybody has an "idea" on how to solve the national debt. Cut welfare! Phase out entitlements! Lower taxes! Close loopholes! Change to a flat tax! Up tariff taxes! Raise tobacco taxes! Institute value added taxes! Reduce the marginal tax rate! Listen to any talk show. The solutions offered are endless, but the only ideas that count are those held by the majority of congressmen and senators. Many who are still in office are the authors of, or voted for, the present tax laws. They have purposefully enlarged the debt. The statutes will remain until the Congress alters its thinking or there is a different Congress, one with sufficient fortitude to withstand the cries of those on the receiving end of government.

It's one thing for a congressional candidate to tell constituents he is willing to cut entitlements, but quite another to tell the mass of recipients who will descend upon his office in Washington. The welfare business will see that the halls of Congress are full of old folks in wheelchairs when the cuts are discussed.

To put it bluntly, ideas count for nothing unless there is a way or will to implement them. To return this country to fiscal sanity will take guts and structure.

The leftists have put wheels under their lousy concepts and have implemented them by the systematic election of their own to public office.

How did they do it? They organize around Marxian class concepts—labor, race, age, etc.,—and seize upon hot class issues. They also form a series of special interest movements. The elitist leadership, working with class interests and special-issue interests forms a series of circles of influence. They then rally their target classes and single-issue interests around their chosen candidate. Knowing that no one special interest group is capable of comprising the majority vote needed to elect, the left combines a number of special interests, each one contributing a percentage to it. Slowly but surely, using this technique, the left has organized and elected their own. The leftist leadership of these separate circles of interest networks with each other, selects one of their own, and elects him. They intentionally keep their special interest membership blissfully ignorant of the overall humanist philosophy of their candidates.

The radical-left hard core is the glue that holds these separate circles of interest together. Rarely, if ever, do the groups' general memberships come in contact with each other, mainly because of the differences they have regarding key issues. This explains how the teamsters and longshoremen unions would support the same candidate as the homosexuals and feminists. This is why many of the patriotic, World War II elderly voted for the same candidate as the radical, pot-smoking Viet Nam demonstrators. The information they receive on the candidate's views speaks only to their own self-interest. By pulling together these circles of special interests on Election Day, leftist candidates garner sufficient votes to win.

Through the organization of these special interest groups, the leftist elite develops new cadre members with leadership potential. Properly indoctrinated, they then spin off, forming new circles of interest. From the activities of these special interests, these ad hoc committees, the new political leadership emerges. Once elected, those who have come up through the leftist ranks introduce the appropriate socialist legislation while the special interest staff does the legwork.

Most legislators are not the intellectual authors of their own legislation, nor do they do most of the work to ensure its passage. Key legislative personnel and the staff of the special interests do the details and the lobbying.

The legislator is, more often than not, just the front man, the spokesman, the shill.

The radical left has been doing the above for seventy-plus years.

The conservative opposition, usually active within the Republican Party, has been a loose collection of traditionalists, irritated by the incremental socialist advance, coming together and occasionally winning. When conservative Republicans are elected, there is no plan of positive confrontation, nor any purpose or resolve to dismantle the incumbent bureaucracy. They run headlong into a minority of elected moderate Republicans who have the silly idea they should run the government "better." All the moderate Republicans have accomplished so far is to manage a larger bureaucracy put in place by past leftist legislation and administrations.

Within the past forty years, some conservatives have gotten smart and started to set up their own special interest groups, networking with others and impacting legislative races. Suddenly, the liberals became agitated and disturbed over the emergence of these new organizations, especially the ones with PACs. What was good for the left-wing goose wasn't good for the right-wing gander. The demand for "campaign reform" was raised, invariably hurting the conservatives while leaving relatively intact the resources and power of leftist groups, specifically the unions.

It's a fact of life, and I'll say it again, only a small percentage of Americans participate in the elective process. Voting in the general elections is the most the vast majority will ever do. What does that tell us? It should tell us that conservatives have to organize differently.

Let's theorize that we split the 5 percent of the people who are political activists into two camps—2.5 percent on the left side and 2.5 percent on the right—the socialist activists against the traditionalists. As I've stressed before, the small percentage of leftists, knowing the public disinterest in politics overall, has successfully organized over the last century around Marxian class concepts—forming laborers and government workers into unions, organizing feminists, students, anti-war pacifists, environmentalists, etc.

What are the conservative activists attempting to do? Are they not trying to educate everyone on every issue? Failing to understand that only a small percentage thinks in political abstracts, they use a shotgun approach, thinking they can swell the conservative ranks, the 2.5 percent, into a majority, 50 percent or more. They keep hoping their educational efforts will enlighten enough people for conservatives to win in the political process. They are attempting the impossible, trying to expand the unexpandable, random shotgunning when rifle shooting is what's needed.

We are not in need of another national conservative group or a new party trying to reinvent the conservative wheel, banding together and then falling apart anew, tripping over the same mistakes while trying to educate everyone on all things. We need a knowledgeable hard core that knows politics, not a groaning band with no realistic goals. We are in need of knowledgeable leadership—forming single-issue structures with good citizens who aren't politically sophisticated, then networking with other leaders to change the political process.

Our strength is in American diversification and individuality.

We don't need one organization focused on everything, but multiple organizations focused on single issues, networking with others at election time, led by confrontationally trained traditional Americans.

The role of our activists must be to identify sensitive, high-intensity issues and provide leadership by forming structures for single-issue-minded people to join. Then, translate that energy into volunteerism and, if possible, professional political action.

The effective combination of multiple "single-issue" groups networking with each other can overpower any combination of those advancing the "class concept" structure. In fact, hot-button topics around which we should and can organize are legion.

With patience and structure, we can cut heavily into the opposition.

One of the advantages of building structure around a given issue is that it is much easier to recruit people into action. Traditionalists need not spend their time trying to convert liberals into conservatives; all they need to do is get single-issue-oriented Americans politically organized. Churchgoers work within the church, gunners organize gunners, businessmen organize businessmen, and young women work with other like-minded women on moral subjects.

The point is, one never has to wander far to be effective. Young parents can gather around educational issues, old folks around fiscal responsibility, farmers around farm issues, veterans around defense—the issues are seemingly endless.

To be effective, we don't have to appear on television debating some slick, greasy-tongued liberal, or go door-to-door handing out literature in some high crime part of town. Provide the money for printing and stamps to mail brochures. Let the post office do the walking. Sponsor, with friends, a neighborhood fundraiser barbecue in a backyard or put together a group yard sale. Clean out the garage for good government.

One doesn't have to confront the humanist crowd in person to be effective. There are plenty of ways to be active without directly scrapping verbally with the bad guys. There are plenty of single-issue white hats to organize and offer moral, political direction.

The humanists, with a small minority of activists, moved into and now dominate the Democratic Party. They are now working their way into the ranks of the Republicans. Are we so inept that we can't do the same? I think not.

14

Dogs, Snakes, Jackasses,
and Leftists

"I thought he was a good guy! He promised he wouldn't vote for new taxes, but it didn't take him long to forget that campaign promise. That dirty rotten turncoat! Talks like a Republican—votes like a Democrat!"

Heard that one before? I have. More times than I can count. The angry commentary is often embellished with a wide variety of Anglo-Saxon expletives. The disgruntled remark is inevitably followed by, "Why would he do that? I thought he really was one of us."

The answer is, he might have been. This disappointment usually comes from someone who doesn't grasp the inner machinations of contemporary politics, especially where legislators serve full time or, in some cases, where legislatures meet annually for many months. It happens much more often with Republicans than with Democrats.

What generally occurs is called a peer-group shift. This is where the constituency shifts from the folks back home to the new friends the legislator makes in the capitol. The time frame will be directly proportional to the shallowness of his ideological commitment, multiplied by the inability of the hometown folks who elected him to keep him in line.

That is why, once he's elected, good staff must surround him and he must be kept in constant contact with those who elected him. In Washington DC and in states with legislatures that meet for long sessions, this requires full-time contact in the Capitol by the organizations that supported him. If the legislator is left alone, surrounded by skilled, affable, highly paid lobbyists, the chances are you will lose him, bit by bit, over a period of time.

To counter this process requires willingness on the part of his constituency to both praise and punish. He has to know that to stray from the path guarantees pain, even loss of office.

In the not-too-distant past, legislatures, including Congress, were part-time. The officeholder earned the bulk of his income at home and his roots were in the district. Serving part-time attracted the most desirable elements of the community to seek office. A full-time legislative job is unattractive to many qualified citizens.

Today, the best people within the Republican ranks don't choose public office as a career, because they already have one. The most capable are content to stay in the free enterprise system.

Not so with liberals. Governmental power attracts them much as flies to decaying meat. They seek public office and government employment; the free market has little appeal to them. In college, they study political science, education, the social sciences, environmental studies, and the law, and then aspire to enter governmental employment. They seek office at local levels, participate in political organizations, are members of leftist special interest groups such as NOW, ACLU (American Civil Liberties Union), MoveOn, DailyKos, and environmental organizations—all with the idea of promoting humanist causes through political power.

Much as in baseball, the left literally develops a farm system where they gain experience and credentials. By the time they run for state office, leftists have developed credible résumés. No neophytes make it to the top of the Democratic heap; no cherries are to be found on the left limb of the legislative tree.

Republicans have no such structure. They usually collect a grab bag of candidates who are often second best. Generally, they sound good and are fairly nice guys, but they are not philosophically well grounded. Too often they lack any practical experience.

Unfortunately, many people who seek office on the Republican side have little philosophical commitment. Their hearts may be in the right place, but their minds are not. I don't make this point lightly. I have interviewed hundreds of candidates over more than 35 years, both as the head of a major political action committee and as my state's senate caucus chairman. I found few who were intellectually capable of defending their conservative views when pressed or were knowledgeable about the opposition's tactics.

Some of the candidates "didn't like what the government was doing." They were viscerally in tune, but surprisingly incapable of intellectually defending the free enterprise system. I've met doctors who can't see the fallacies of socialized medicine, insurance salesmen who have little knowledge of economics, and contractors who don't mind crippling regulations. Being successful in business is no proof that one can be successful in political office.

In contemporary politics, those desiring elective employment are not introverts. You do not find shy people seeking office. Inevitably, those who win elections have oversized egos.

It takes a high opinion of one's ability to endure the rigors of campaigning. These men and women view themselves as leaders who "can turn it all around." To put it succinctly, they have a high opinion of themselves and invariably are susceptible to praise. They bask in the attention, enjoying the adoration given to elected officials. They look forward to the limelight that accompanies public office and, once attained, they hate to lose it. Therefore, they tend to avoid taking positions on controversial issues and dislike confrontation. This is much more true of Republicans than Democrats.

The people who are philosophically committed to humanism know that criticism will be forthcoming when they pursue confrontation. That's why they gravitate to elective office—to make change. Humanists advocate continual social change, knowing controversy goes with the territory. The well-grounded conservative is ideologically committed to dismantling the socialism already in place but, as discussed, rarely understands the nature of the battle needed to achieve that end.

Compare most legislators to people in other professions. Most legislators have much in common with movie actors. Both are given inordinate attention by the public, love basking in the limelight, enjoy hamming it up and performing before audiences, delight in the favorable attention of the media and develop a high opinion of their own importance. Because of these and other less admirable human characteristics, most have to be watched at all times. When newly elected legislators find themselves voting on the expenditure of billions of dollars, surrounded by sophisticated special interests who hang on their every word, is it any surprise that some weaken? The less ideologically grounded they are, the quicker their clay feet sink under the ooze of adulation.

Conservatives rarely threaten or discipline an incumbent who strays far from the issues that elected him. Who's to punish incumbents? Who's to hold them accountable? Most business and conservative organizations are defensive, by definition only wishing to be left alone, not willing to rock anyone's political canoe. Holding a once-friendly legislator's feet to the fire is not the modus operandi of most conservative organizations. Certainly none of the official Republican organizations would dare to intimidate an incumbent—or even want to. And if a local Republican leader or elected official speaks out in condemnation of a wayward fellow Republican, the party often threatens to revoke his or her Republican credentials.

I am an admirer of former California Governor Ronald Reagan. But his so-called Eleventh Commandment, "Never speak ill of another Republican," protects only philosophically drifting incumbents.

Not so on the liberal side. Step out of line, and expect the worst. As explained in earlier chapters, the Democrats in office are heavily influenced by the radical hardcore leadership in the public employee unions, NEA, trial lawyers, homosexual activists, various so-called "public interest" groups, et al. These and others play a major role in calling the political tune. These special interests, by the nature of their employment, are ever present in the capitol. The unions threaten, intimidate, and punish those who dare to stray far from left field. They will, however, pragmatically let a legislator cast an occasional contrary vote if his district is vulnerable. But, stray too far and the Democrat faces a heavily supported primary opponent in the next election.

Since Republicans rarely oust one of their own and external pressure from conservative groups is with few exceptions to date negligible, it is easy for the elected Republican to stray. The outside pressures are ever present. Add the traditional American desire to avoid confrontation and the lack of internal party discipline, and many wander into greener left-wing pastures. The liberal is ever ready to exploit the elected Republican's desire to be liked with soothing comments like, "You're not like those other right-wing conservatives. You're sensible. We can deal with you."

Lacking knowledge of confrontational skills, our elected "freedom fighter" slips from conservative grace on the oily tongue of liberalism.

"He used to be such a good guy!"

Maybe he was. But more likely, he didn't have a strong enough philosophical core to resist the pressure applied by so many of those inhabiting the capitol halls. We often elect "one of us," then send him off to be constantly surrounded by "a bunch of them." Massive sums are paid to those who can influence the legislature. There are at least ten lobbyists for every one legislator.

It is not uncommon for a decent man to be wined, dined, and schmoozed by lobbyists and his Democratic colleagues until his judgment becomes so impaired that he loses all perspective about what is real and what is false. It takes a strong, ideologically well-grounded person to withstand the pressure year after year. It requires constant contact by those who elected him. Few amateur groups have the ability to have volunteers at the capitol keeping an eye on what's going on. Out of necessity, they must raise the funds to hire someone full-time to do what they cannot. Successful professional organizations do just that. They hire or train watchdogs to monitor those they elect.

Contemporary legislative bodies aren't debating forums where intellectuals gather to seek out the truth, where ideas are challenged and differing opinions respected. To the contrary, in a legislature where liberalism has a foothold, dogma is skillfully forced down the throats of the opposition, amidst sufficient propaganda to placate the uninformed. It isn't a forum for logic and reason, but an arena of simple addition. If you can count up the necessary votes, your "logic" wins.

During the twenty-two years I served in the California state senate, only once did a member of the Democrat party show any curiosity in the logical genesis of my argument—once in twenty-two years! Debate is for public consumption—for the press corps and for TV coverage. Today, debate rarely has much to do with deciding the final outcome of the vote.

One of the more humorous sides of floor debates is that the more vocal and prolonged the discussion, the more assured is the outcome before the debate even begins. Only on the most inconsequential legislation does floor debate have even the slightest impact on the final vote. Rarely is a colleague's mind altered by the pearls of wisdom that dribble from a legislator's lips.

Unfortunately, the vapid air that flows from the left influences many a naïve soul when reading the press. A lot of our politically Pollyannaish friends often say, "Oh, he may be a liberal but every once in a while he does something right and votes with us on our issue." Or, "He may be liberal, but he is such a nice guy."

So what? We should remind them that Lucifer, the fallen angel, was the most handsome of all. Being congenial and appearing reasonable are tools of the political trade; without them, no officeholder is around very long.

Remember, an average Democrat with conservative ideas doesn't get elected to high office. He wouldn't get the time of day from the left-wingers who control the party apparatus.

Those who make it into office are carefully chosen and selected because of their liberalism or willingness to mouth the line, not in spite of it.

Once in office, the lefty may represent a district where, if his views were widely known, he would possibly lose. In order to protect his backside, the left allows a few conservative crumbs to fall from his plate, hoping they will be gobbled-up by the gullible gentry. They usually are.

The left-wing legislator, if his district isn't totally safe, will often pick a conservative issue and sound like one of its champions—not enough to make any difference, but with sufficient vigor to convince the gullible folks back home that he is on their side. Such action is usually nothing more than protective coloration, conservative camouflage. However, behind the scenes—out of daily view from his constituency—he works diligently to undermine the position he just voted for.

"Tough on crime" rhetoric is standard fare. Match such rhetoric against contributions received from the left. The leftist politician, with public fanfare, votes for the death penalty and then marches in step with the Trial Lawyers and the ACLU on every measure that counteracts his vote.

Abortion is another legislative issue where duplicity raises its head. One senator convinced the pro-life people he was one of them and, on highly visible votes, would be by their side. However, when he finally attained leadership and could use his office to advance pro-life issues, nothing positive took place. In fact, the opposite occurred. While appointing rabid pro-abortionists to key committees, he fired those staff members who were pro-life and retained the pro-abort activists.

A liberal congressman, while serving on the national board of the National Rifle Association (NRA) voted for banning semi-automatic firearms. For years he had convinced fellow board members he was one of them, a first-class pro-gun advocate. But when the left really needed him, he cast a crucial anti-gun vote and used his position as an NRA board member to sway other congressmen.

Christ warned that we will, "Know them by their fruits"—by what they do, not what they say. Actions DO speak louder than words. If a certain legislator is a left-wing lemon producer, be highly suspect when he offers up a right-wing apple. The hard-core politicos see that most voters haven't the time to watch the inner machinations of the legislature. They get a big laugh from planning and then implementing their culpable capers.

Liberal legislators practice deceit. It's well within their ethics to do so. Why bother to get excited when viewing them on television or listening to them pontificate on talk shows? Why get frustrated and an ulcerated tummy over something which we should expect? By their nature and training they will omit key information, color their commentaries with personally clever anecdotes, and tell outright fibs if necessary. Why be upset by their propaganda and clutter our brains worrying over their nonsensical left-wing trivia? Dogs bark, snakes wiggle, jackasses bray, vultures vomit, and radical leftists lie. It's their nature to do so.

Listening to C-SPAN won't tell us much unless we know the players. Why clutter the brain with political gunk? Whenever anyone asks my opinion of Speaker Pelosi's or some other liberal's last speech, I tell them I'm not into fiction so I didn't watch it—and I didn't. Why get upset watching prevaricators prevaricate?

I'm in the business of raising THEIR blood pressure.

I am a giver of ulcers, not a getter. Shouldn't you be, too?

15

No More Old, Depressing, Conservative Games— It's Time to Have Fun

To be effective, positive confrontation requires a positive attitude. Is it important? Very. Karl Marx knew it, Lenin knew it, Dale Carnegie knew it, but many conservatives don't seem to get the message. Too many conservatives seem to bask in the game of "One-downs-man-ship."

The way this game is played is to gather with others of like mind, then relate some nasty thing the liberals have recently done. You can bet your Ollie North watch someone will try to tell a more ghastly story. It soon becomes a feeding frenzy of gloomies; one gut-wrenching story after another spills forth, until someone tells of an event no one can top. Amidst groans, curled lips, and rolled-up eyes the game stops with everyone being totally depressed and thinking of buying another year's supply of survival food. The winner, of course, is the last story-teller. This is, undoubtedly, the conservative's favorite sport. At almost any gathering of Republicans you can find several groups of philosophically committed conservatives deeply engaged in depressing each other. The party pooper is the odd fellow who talks about winning and explains how it can be done.

It's small wonder that the conservatives have been a minority for so many years; a wake is often more joyful than attending one of their meetings. Their fundraising dinners are usually the epitome of travail. The tickets are costly, the fare is fair, and a speaker with a masters degree in one-downs-man-ship inevitably follows the dessert with one gloomy anecdote after another. The speaker soon ulcerates whatever small pleasure the food may have produced. I have often thought the speaker should talk before dinner. Better yet, before anyone shows up. A synopsis of his dissertation could be tucked under the salad plate for any masochists in attendance.

Victory is what politics is all about, and how to win should be on every good guy's mind. There are only so many hours in a day. Why waste them on gloomy thoughts when we should be concentrating on giving the socialists fits? We could take a lesson from some dead lefties whose ideas are still alive in the minds of tenured, albeit demented, college professors. Karl Marx dreamed up a lot of hateful tripe—but, all of his ideas weren't totally crazy. One of his more popular themes was, "Comrades, socialism and then communism—IT'S INEVITABLE!" He then composed a "scientific" theory that proved his "inevitability" point for eggheads, naive students, and mentally slow academicians.

What a smart sales tool! Think about it—just convince all your little left-leaning lemmings that history is your ally, that communism is the wave of the future, preordained, and chiseled in stone. What could stand in the way, since history and science have promised victory? Believing you are going to win is a great confidence builder. And being told you are an integral part of creating a New World Order is heady stuff indeed.

A rational look at the past clearly shows Marx was hallucinating, since the opposite has occurred. Liberty has been the upward path of mankind, not totalitarianism. Growth of personal freedom and the establishment of democratic institutions has been history's overall trend. However, like the stock market, freedom's advancement hasn't been straight up. It has suffered its share of ups and downs, evolutionary and devolutionary movements. Although serfdom has been around for centuries, no one with a modicum of common sense believes it's a growth industry. Freedom, not slavery, continues on the rise. In his monumental four-volume work, *The History of the English Speaking Peoples,* Winston Churchill's closing words are, "The future is unknowable, but the past should give us hope." And indeed it should. The struggle of mankind has been a twisted path of upward reach.

Within the past few decades, the morals of America have been slipping backward. But it is comforting to know that history is on our side and logic and the lessons of the ages doom the socialists. Let's concentrate on how we can speed up the process of freedom and reverse this regressive quackery.

First, let's learn a bit from the past.

Marx's ideas had little impact on anyone until Vladimir Lenin came along and put organizational wheels under Karl's madness. Vladimir laid out the structure, explaining how a tiny minority could wreak havoc and gain power. He was right. For close to a century we have seen how organization and dedication can implement bad ideas, especially when good ideas are languishing and taken for granted. Ideas are like eggs, they either develop and hatch or rot.

This tells us once more that with a modicum of organizational effort and dedication by a relative few, liberty can once more prosper. But first, we must get off of the one-downs-man-ship kick. That doesn't mean we should stop discussing leftists' foolishness and what chicanery they are up to. But we should analyze their weaknesses and look for vulnerabilities. We should probe their mistakes, find their Achilles' heel and use the issue to find new allies who just had their hot button pushed. Then, we must influence them into joining the fight, registering to vote, and contributing to the cause.

When I first became aware the country was morally headed in the wrong direction, I engaged daily in another favorite conservative ploy called "leftist box watching." The way you play this game is to read what the opposition is doing and then keep track, on a chart, of all the left-wing activists and what organizations they join. Draw a box around each active radical lefty. When you find another group they have lent their name to, draw a line connecting the two. The worst liberal is the one in the most boxes with the most lines drawn to him. Watching activist lefties can keep you real busy, angry, and frustrated. Before long you discover that the same names keep cropping up over and over. I said to myself, "Hey, there can't be a lot of left-wingers calling the shots if they have to belong to so many groups."

Then, two things dawned on me. There are not really that many hard-core leftists, so why should I spend so much time watching them? Why don't I do something positive and have *them* watch *me?* If I'm spending all of my time boxing socialists' names, I'm not spending enough hours giving them trouble. I then set my goal to be in a box or two and be a watchee instead of a watcher.

Years later, a friend sent me a chart constructed by a local left-wing activist. There I was—right in the middle of the chart with lines connecting me with some of the heavy hitters on our side! What acclaim! That lefty must have spent weeks digging up all that information. I felt a little slighted, however, since he had missed a few big names. I felt like sending him a letter pointing out the omissions. But then again, why do the bugger's work for him? As long as he's busy watching us good guys, he's not promoting some new socialist machination. The day the leftists spend most of their time watching us is the day we start to win. There are only so many hours in a day, and how we good guys spend them is all-important.

Think long and hard about it. There is only so much productive time. Isn't it better dedicating your hours to giving the other side trouble than stewing and complaining over what they are doing to us?

Are we in any boxes with lines leading this way or that, or are we just a watcher of those who are in the parade? Are we in any organization that is giving the left apoplexy? Do humanists blubber at the mention of our names or the organizations we support?

Personally, I'm out to get into more boxes. How about you? If you're not, why not do something about it? Don't you think it's better to give political pain than to receive it?

Many conservatives suffer under the misconception that fighting confrontationally requires the use of dirty tactics. They think that in order to win we must be like our opposition.

Nothing of the sort—the more honest and ethical you are, the better your chances of winning. St. Paul tells us, "Repay no one evil for evil." Politics need not be dirty, dishonest or unethical. The end does **NOT** justify the means, but it's a fact that the end product is shaped by the means used to get there.

It's silly to expect a good person to be elected to office by foul trickery and not to have compromised his principles in the process. Unethical or deceitful people do not elect honest candidates.

That does not mean we shouldn't be aware of the impending confrontation or be surprised by the existence of chicanery, half-truths, and outright prevarication that exists in contemporary politics. Those who have situational ethics will easily lie if it benefits their interests and they believe they can get away with it. Remember, dogs bark, jackasses bray, snakes wiggle, and liberals lie; it's their nature to do so. Exposing a liar is confrontational. They first deny, then change the subject, then attack the accuser's character. The more vigorously we pursue the truth, the louder they scream.

These anguished outcries are often intended to intimidate and cause us to desist. Those reared with the Christian ethic tend to back off and give the liar the benefit of the doubt when the yelling begins. Bad move. Their cries of anguish are confirmation that we're on the right course. This is the time to forge ahead and press on. It's time to rejoice. The outcry is, in fact, proof this confrontation is working for you. No need to get angry or nasty in return when being confrontational. In fact, the more in control and the calmer we remain, the better. Be persistent, tenacious, and firm.

A number of years ago, Barbara, a fine, but sorely distressed, Christian activist came into my office with tears streaming down her cheeks. She had been working the capitol halls, lobbying for legislation requiring parental consent for abortions on their minor children. She was no ordinary gal. She had organized a powerful group of women around this issue. One senator was the key to moving the bill out of committee, and the phone calls to his office had been voluminous. He was infuriated and extremely nervous over the pressure placed upon him. When he saw Barbara in the hall, he angrily berated her, calling her filthy names and loudly denouncing the phone call blitz.

Barbara was shocked by his behavior and was convinced they had overdone the pressure. She was stunned as I smiled from ear to ear and exclaimed, "You got him!"

I knew the senator was a closet liberal, holding a marginal seat. I thought he would dialectically move backward under pressure. His anger was proof positive it was working.

Barbara wasn't so sure, so she requested I be present when the bill was heard before committee. She was convinced that when she testified on the bill he would tear her apart.

During the committee hearing, the angry solon sat mutely in his chair, an ugly scowl split his fat face. He didn't say anything until the vote was called. Then, he said just one word, saturated in bile, "AAAagh-aye." Out came the bill.

A few years later we elected that wonderful woman to the state assembly. The experience and contacts she gained while working the capitol halls made her one of our best.

Often people have said to me, "Promoting your political beliefs must have brought you under constant attack when you were a legislator."

They have all been surprised by my response, "No, hardly at all."

Personal attacks have been minimal because I looked forward to them, sometimes even enjoyed them and often exploited the attacks to my advantage. I receive satisfaction from knowing that my efforts are causing political pain. It didn't take long before the left figured it out and quit. Who likes to make their enemy happy?

Their attacks expanded my base of contacts and rallied more friends to my side. The left can attack me for being strong on law enforcement, pro-life, pro-gun, pro-God. They can go ahead and attack away to their heart's content. However, they're smart enough not to.

I've related to many a conservative friend that they will never know their effectiveness until they're attacked by some big left-winger. When it happens—enjoy—have a party.

Some time ago, the feminist group NOW (National Organization for Women), hoping to intimidate me, called to inform me I had been given the "Chauvinist of the Year" award. They wanted to come to my office right away to present it to me. I told them I'd be delighted, but could they put it off for at least an hour, so I could round up the press.

They never showed up, but they sent it to me through the mail. It proudly hangs on our laundry room wall.

When dealing with the other side, it doesn't pay, nor is it wise, to be belligerent, haughty, or mean-spirited. We can be firm, tenacious, and unwilling to compromise, even with smiles on our faces. Sublimating our inner anger over the effrontery of the opposition is a smart tactic. We are biblically cautioned to be "wise as serpents and harmless as doves."

The left is totally unaccustomed to facing a smiling, confident conservative—especially one who won't allow himself to be put on the defensive, one who doesn't waste time basking in the critical gloom of one-downs-man-ship.

We must be combatants and doers, always remembering the words of Theodore Roosevelt, "It is not the critic who counts; not the man who points out how the strong man stumbles, or where the doer of deeds could have done better. The credit belongs to the man who is actually in the arena, whose face is marred by dust and sweat and blood; who strives valiantly, who errs, and comes short again and again, because there is no effort without error and shortcoming; but who does actually strive to do the deeds."

This rugged president also said, "Far better it is to dare mighty things, to win glorious triumphs, even though checkered by failure, than to take rank with those poor spirits who neither enjoy much nor suffer much because they live in the gray twilight that knows neither victory nor defeat."

Wise and inspirational words, don't ya' think?

16

How Not to Live the Party Life

The general public believes the Democrat and the Republican parties are the political leadership of the country. Far from it. In reality, both are better defined as large social clubs for political groupies, fundraising fronts, and media outlets. In fact, both structures are little more than a means of legally registering to vote and a haven for big-salary political hacks who squander most dollars given them. Both parties are perennially in debt.

There is no litmus test given upon joining a political party, no loyalty oath, nor commitment to any specific course of action. To register in either party, all you have to be is eighteen and warm. In some states with lax registration laws and laggard enforcement, even being warm isn't a necessity.

Both parties have clubs and party affiliations where a person can join to associate with other political groupies. Some of these party groups endorse in the primaries and serve worthwhile functions. Others are no more than paper structures. Some of the party faithful register voters and turn out votes on election day. Sometimes they even perform this function adequately, but neither party is the driving force behind policy once their choices are elected. Party platforms are blissfully ignored. The Republican Party rarely punishes its officeholders who go astray. The party structures don't even usually select or help candidates in the primaries and, under some states' laws, are prohibited from doing so. They have to wait until candidate selection is accomplished by sophisticated special interests who have no such restrictions. Political parties are, by nature, eunuchs, incapable of impregnating any worthwhile ideas in anyone. At conventions, they are nothing more than platforms of blather and blab.

On the Democrat side, the people who get the action from officeholders are the special interest leadership. They punish and they reward. Thus, they are listened to. They father candidates in primaries, give them money, and are the real sires of political action.

The labor unions are a leading example of those who know how to inflict pain. With less than 10 percent of the total workforce unionized, they are powerfully influential on all legislative bodies. Their leadership knows how to use their clout and remind politicos with short memories as to where their money, troops, and votes come from.

The homosexuals are another effective political interest. With a very small segment of the population, their high-pitched political voice is loudly heard.

Contrast that with the Christian community, which constitutes vast numbers of citizens. Policy-wise they are largely ignored and often vilified. Until recently, their voices have been barely a soft murmur. Fearing the latent power that exists within the faithful, the left preemptively strikes against members of the religious community, seeking to mute their voices. They have had a surprising degree of success, dissuading many Christians from wandering out of their pews. Most just piously pray and delegate to God all political action. Others are quickly energized to work and vote for a favored politician (or against a disfavored one), and then just as quickly go back to political sleep. Meanwhile the favored, and now safely elected, politician begins the inevitable peer-group shift to the left.

In need not stay this way.

In the early 1920s, the Democrat Party was in disarray, a feeble force in America. The humanists, socialists, communists, and leftist intellectuals abandoned the socialist parties and found ripe pickings in the Democrat structure. The union movement was a special interest vehicle they seized and controlled. Using the union movement effectively and exploiting the travail that prevailed during the Great Depression, they capitalized on the anguish to consolidate their hold on the Democrat Party.

Slowly but surely, they systematically gained control of party leadership. They focused their attention on the populous northern states. By the early '60s, the radicals had gained a majority of the Democrats in Congress, wrestling power away from the more conservative southern Democrats, thereby leveraging the entire Democratic body.

Although they had attained dominance in the Democrat ranks, impacting the one party wasn't enough. Leveraging both parties has always been the goal of the left. The Republicans have been more difficult to dominate since their rank and file have historically been basically conservative, supporters of the status quo with a more affluent membership. Nevertheless, the left has been successful, to a debilitating degree, electing a few "Republicans" who are outright liberals and "moderates," who constantly stand in the way of any attempt to cut back aggressively on the incumbent bureaucracy.

The leftist Republicans are always meekly willing to compromise and give up more ground to the leftist Democrats. But within the Republican caucus, they are extremely aggressive and antagonistic in opposition to the conservatives. The reason is simple: Their ethics and political persuasion are barely distinguishable from those of the Democrat humanists.

The conflict, therefore, is not between Republicans and Democrats; it's between conservatives and liberals—traditional American values adherents against humanists.

Both parties are mere platforms of babble and blab, but one must register in order to vote. Giving one's total loyalty to either party is foolishness. The selection of which party to register in must be a pragmatic choice. Within which party can the conservative do the most good?

At the present time, the Republican structure is where the conservative has the best ability to consolidate control. At present time, the opportunities for leverage are far greater there than in the Democrat Party.

The Republican surge during the 1990s gained control of the U.S. Senate and Congress. Because this control was not wisely used, the control of Congress slipped from their grasp. It is time for the leadership to move into the hands of confrontationally wise, traditional American conservatives. When this is accomplished, the liberal Republicans should be isolated, ignored, and when practical, systematically replaced. This is what the liberal Democrats did to the conservative Democrats. As long as they were useful in maintaining the majority, they were tolerated and, if possible, isolated. But whenever the opportunity arose, the liberal leadership quietly and efficiently replaced them. The liberals never forget it's a numbers game. The one who has the numbers wins.

Party loyalty has its place. It houses the faithful who vote for their party through thick and thin, regardless of the qualifications of the candidate. Each district has its bowsers and they should be identified as an element in every election, since party loyalty is their hot button. In many cases it's not so much that they love their own party but that they hate the other. These rather narrow folks are called "yellow dogs" because they would vote for a yellow dog rather than vote for the other party. This feeling runs very deep in some people, but fortunately, not in most. My great-grandfather, a solid rock Republican, would not permit my grandmother to marry her first love because he was a Democrat. Several of my uncles idolized Franklin D. Roosevelt and wouldn't dream of voting Republican.

This dislike for the opposite party is not uncommon. I ran across it with some regularity while serving in office. The intensity of it in some folks is rather unnerving and sometimes humorous. Once, at a cocktail party, I was introduced to the mother of the host. She was a small prune-faced old lady whose sour countenance was exceeded only by her lack of civility.

"Mama, I'd like you to meet Senator Richardson." The old gal cocked her head, curled her lip and inquired in an acidic tone, "What are ya', Republican or Democrat?"

"I'm a Republican," I responded, turning on my most charming, never-fail, vote-getting smile.

"I wouldn't vote fer a Republican if ya' were the last man on earth," she spat out while leaning menacingly in my direction.

Not to be intimidated, I continued with my most engaging grin and asked, "If Joe Stalin ran as a Democrat against a moral Republican would you still vote for him?"

Without hesitation she shot back, "You bet I would!"

I knew the hostess was a Christian so I assumed her mother was also. I piously asked her, "What if ole Joe Stalin was running against Saint Paul, a Republican?"

This time she did hesitate, but only to screw up her face, raise one eyebrow to her hairline while dropping the other to her chin. "I'd still vote for Joe," she venomously enunciated.

I would call that old gal a yellow dog Democrat.

On another occasion, a good pal of mine was seeking a seat in the California state assembly. The district was heavily Democrat. My friend, Gordon Browning, was a sergeant in the Los Angeles police department. While going door-to-door ringing doorbells he was rudely confronted by an obese housefrau, hair up in curlers and still in her housecoat.

"What do you want?" she suspiciously inquired. The screen door was slightly ajar and around her fireplug legs darted a small monkey which quickly attached itself to Gordon's leg and attempted to bite him through his pants.

Gordon, being one of Los Angeles's finest, ignored the little varmint and began his pitch. "How do you do, madam, my name is Gordon Browning and I'm running for . . . ."

She rudely interrupted, "What are ya', Republican or Democrat?"

"Well, I'm a Republican."

Again, using the same old yellow-dog response, "I wouldn't vote for ya' if you wuz the last man on earth!"

"That is your prerogative ma'am. It is a free country. But lady, could I ask a favor of you?"

"What's that?" she suspiciously asked.

"Would you ask your child to let go of my leg?"

In order to show yellow-dogism isn't a one-party phenomenon, here is another anecdote. In Vermont, Miss Tillie was the town's most ardent Republican. For seventy years she had voted the straight party line, never varying one iota from the party of Lincoln. You can imagine the shock when everyone in town learned that Miss Tillie had reregistered as a Democrat. A town meeting was called to discuss this momentous event. All could only guess, but none knew why the past president of the state Republican Women's Club and perennial delegate to the Republican National Convention would do such a scandalous thing. Finally a committee was formed to ask Miss Tillie why the change of heart. Why did she switch from elephants to donkeys?

The delegation, made up of the leading citizens, phoned for an appointment. Bright and early the next morning, they all were seated in Miss Tillie's living room, brimming with curiosity. After polite formalities, the mayor summoned the courage to ask the question.

Miss Tillie demurely replied, "Well, last week I was feeling rather poorly so I went to see my doctor. The news was not good, and he told me I had but a few months to live. I figured if I had to go, I'd rather it be one of them instead of one of us."

Proper polling can identify the yellow dogs in any district. The object is to maximize the turn out of your own bowsers and try not to agitate the canary-colored mongrels on the other side. They are the last people you want receiving the literature of your favorite candidate. It's better they don't know a competitive election exists because it tends to galvanize them into action, making Rottweilers out of shaggy, yellow puppies.

Unless there's a major disaster, comparable to the '20s, no third party has much of a chance of success. In fact, third parties most of the time only hurt the Republican side. Americans, for close to two centuries, have been comfortable with the two-party system. Disenchanted at times, but still satisfied. Besides, special interests have too much invested in the Democrat Party to switch to another. On the conservative side, the opportunity to control the Republican structure is a reality and within sight. To abandon that goal for a third party would be a calculated waste of time and money.

Third-party attempts distract primarily from the Republican side, prolonging conservative attempts to be the dominant voice within the Republican structure. Third-party efforts have little impact on the Democrats since their organizational control over the special interests under their umbrella is hardly affected. Third-party efforts are for the unsophisticated and politically gullible, usually those who are new to politics, libertines, and those looking for, and desiring, a fast fix. Sadly, it is also home to some well-intentioned activists who give up after a few failures or ugly incidents within the Republican Party.

One need do no more than objectively study the ineffectiveness of the Perot movement or the machinations of the Libertarians to see their negative impact on the conservative movement. Liberals delight in both movements since they know full well how both Perotites and Libertarians have helped the reelection of many a left-wing Democrat incumbent.

It's worth saying once more—politics is a numbers game. Ignore the numbers, and you lose.

Is a successful third party possible? Yes, when all the circumstances are right. What would be needed is a national calamitous event of disastrous ramifications coupled with outstanding national leadership deserting both political parties. It would take a real shock to jar Americans loose from the present two-party system.

But why should we even bother thinking about third parties?

Conservatives have a good foothold in the Republican ranks. With patience, applied confrontation, and a strong stomach, the traditional American can rule the Republican roost and, in time, perhaps the Democrat roost as well.

How? By establishing structure and understanding confrontation.

It may sound like a contradiction, but the situation will sometimes need to get worse in order to get better.

The leftists are in power positions in education, the media, and the bowels of government. They won't go away easily. They will continue to promote their programs while thinking up new excuses to socialize America. They have an immense self-interest in protecting the government programs they have created. Of course, they will justify the use of state power to thwart any opposition. Each time they are heavy-handed, they place opportunities before us. A lot of sleepy Americans will be angrily awakened, constituting a powerful body—if we organize them politically.

17

Let's Stop Just Playing Defense and Roll Some Big Snowballs

I magine one winter day you see a large snowball rolling down the hill, gaining in size and momentum, ultimately threatening your farmhouse. You immediately begin to build a bulwark to stop the snowball's destructive advance. What if halfway through building the bulwark you observe another snowball headed for the barn? Another bulwark? Oops, there's another one threatening the chicken coop!

You would soon become exhausted trying to stop all the snowballs that someone is sending off the top of the hill. Even though every attempt to stop the snowballs succeeded, you would have expended enormous energy and materials. Eventually, some day or night, a big snowball would get through.

Snowballs do not create themselves. Sooner or later you figure out someone is on the hilltop packing small snowballs and rolling them down the hill in your direction, gaining in size. What to do? First, recognize you have an enemy bent on your farm's destruction. Second, realize it's that nasty neighbor down the road, the one who wrote a book about how he intended to take over the farms around the hill.

Several courses of action might be taken. Acknowledge at once that you can't do it alone. So, gather your good neighbors around to help build better barricades and convince them snowballs can be stopped. Then, raise funds and build a snowball smasher. Design an early warning system by hiring full-time, on-the-job lookouts as snowball watchers. Start a newspaper condemning snowball makers.

Better yet, instead of being on the defensive, use leverage. Go half way up the hill and divert the snowball's momentum before it gets too big. Redirect it toward that bad neighbor's farmhouse. It will take less energy and reap for you a lot of positive good. Use the momentum of his snowball to build your special interest strength. Even better, get to the top of the hill and pack your own icy missiles.

The evil neighbor now has to stop making snowballs, tend to his own farm and build a defensive bulwark to protect his own vested interests. You may severely damage his property and dampen his enthusiasm to make any more snowballs.

Initiating an action takes less energy than does a comprehensive reaction. The aggressor has a plan of action, while the one under attack must defend a broader front in order to protect himself. Any lawyer will confirm that being on the defensive is a more difficult assignment than initiating an action. No war is won on the defense, but that is where most traditional Americans are now, fighting a losing, retreating fight.

You need not be stuck on the defensive, especially when the humanists are so vulnerable on so many fronts.

The socialist programs initiated in America are failing as they failed in Eastern Europe. Socialism is based on inaccurate assumptions, fallacious premises, and a misunderstanding of the nature and origin of man. Socialism can survive only if subsidized by the free market system and then, just for so long. It will, like the parasite it is, kill the host unless exterminated. It can be defeated. The quest for power, the excessive taxation needed to feed it, the bureaucracy it creates, the injustice it promotes, the regulatory excesses, and the desire for arbitrary control over all human action create dedicated enemies.

The task then is to politicize those who have been exposed to humanist excesses. Band them together, raise money from them, teach them the strategy of confrontational politics, build residuals, and form PACs. Then your political organization snowballs.

Form these counter organizations around specific issues, after identifying the segments of citizens affected.

Already, numerous groups have been set up to stop some of the socialist power grabs. However, most have been nothing more than barricade builders, attempting to keep themselves from being buried in humanist snow jobs.

It's time to select target districts, networking with like-minded groups who share the goal. Then, together we can work our way to the top of the hill and make our own icy missiles.

Speaking of hills, the biggest snowballs are made in Washington DC on Capitol Hill.

Many years ago, a European correspondent told me that total socialism is the ultimate aim of leftist forces. He thought their chance of succeeding in the United States was slim. "Americans," he said, "are an independent, optimistic, and freedom-loving people. They are like quicksilver. When cupped in the hand, it will hold together, but try to grab it tightly and it will separate and leak out between the fingers." He believed Americans wouldn't be caught in the tightened grip of socialism. I believe he is right.

We Americans are optimists, fiercely independent, and certainly not willing to tolerate a socialist bit in our mouths, attempting to guide us this way and that. Our third president, Thomas Jefferson stated, "... mankind has not been born with the saddles on their backs, nor a favored few booted and spurred ready to ride them legitimately."

Americans will never tolerate a saddle, much less the tight cinch needed to keep on a saddle and rider. I intend this book to cast some light upon how to buck off the saddle blanket, the covering which we were told was only to keep us secure and warm but is, in fact, the first step to being ridden.

We all have much to be thankful for. We've been blessed to live in this stately mansion called America. We did little to deserve it. We were just fortunate enough to be born here or had the opportunity to move in. Only by the grace of God and the hard work of our forefathers do we find ourselves free Americans.

This palatial estate where we reside has countless rooms, including a great kitchen with a full larder. It has beautiful gardens and pathways amidst grand oaks. Tall stately pines surround it. The United States is, without question, the best and most beautiful place on earth.

However, like all structures it must be constantly maintained. Unfortunately, it's been neglected and taken for granted. The caretaker and some of the groundskeepers need to be fired. They haven't taken the job seriously, and they've let it fall into disrepair. The roof now leaks, the outside walls are in need of paint and the foundation needs to be shored up before it topples over. The second mortgage is too large, not to mention the first.

Like many others, I feel obligated to pay it down, then get on with the repairs so we may pass this home on, intact, free and clear, to our children and grandchildren. In the meantime, wouldn't it be nice if we could improve the property by planting some roses along the driveway and cull out the noxious weeds growing and smothering the garden and yard? We could even polish the brass, paint the steps, repair the welcome mat, and leave it looking like new.

Then, when strangers pass by, their jaws would drop in wonderment. Gazing in awe upon our beautiful, stately mansion, they couldn't help but say, "My, the people who live there certainly do take care of it. They must really love that place."

Losing Arguments?
Try Reading *Slightly to the Right*

May we ask a few personal questions of you? Are you one of our fellow conservative Christian friends who have difficulty discussing important political issues with your neighbors, family, and fuzzy friends? Do you find yourself on the defensive with your liberal acquaintances? Do your ears burn red, as your blood begins to boil soon after the conversation begins?

Wouldn't it be nice to win discussions for a change? If so, may we offer a suggestion? It just might help if you read *Slightly to the Right*—a book that has helped many others. Rep. Dana Rohrabacher (R-CA) read the book when he was a young man.

Very recently he said, "Bill Richardson's *Slightly to the Right* was the can-do handbook for generations of conservative activists, including yours truly. He showed conservatives how to be principled without being dogmatic, informative without being burdensome. Bill Richardson had a great political career as a champion of freedom, even more important he equipped a whole generation of young patriots to pick up the load and follow in his footsteps."

Slightly to the Right was written in the beginning of the 1960s, when the threat of Communist subversion was more than just talk. There was hardly any organized conservative movement.

Yet following those gloomy days, the conservative movement fought its way to victory with the election of Ronald Reagan in 1980. A quarter of a million copies of *Slightly to the Right* guided conservatives on how to win. *Slightly to the Right* is needed for today's conservatives to once again retake the initiative and build another road to victory.

There is a whole crop of new conservatives who might want to learn how to be more effective in discussing issues with their less informed acquaintances. Reading this book could help them.

So, download it and enjoy! It's free!
Read the book: http://senhlr.blogspot.com/

What Makes You Think We Read the Bills?

Do you wonder why your congressman says one thing at home and acts differently with his fellow legislators?

This is nothing new. Thirty years ago, California Senator H. L. Richardson wrote *What Makes You Think We Read the Bills?* The situation has not changed much today ... even when it comes to their own bills!

So why do your representatives suddenly stop being your representatives? It's called "Peer-Group Shift," and it starts happening almost as soon as they get elected. Speaking of elections, how do your elected officials get selected? Do majorities elect? You may be surprised with the answer.

With humor and straight talk, Richardson gives concerned citizens a handbook for understanding—and dealing with— their legislators. It's also a lot of fun, with a hilarious introduction by comic Mark Russell.

This is a book that politicians hope you will not read. To encourage you to read it, it is priced at only $4.95 (plus $5.95 shipping and handling) at the Gun Owners of America bookstore (http://www.gunowners.com/bookst.htm).

Please send me a copy of *What Makes You Think We Read the Bills?*

☐ I am enclosing my check for $10.90 (which includes shipping and handling). Please call for shipping and handling rates for multiple copies: (703) 321-8585.

Name _____

Address _____

City/State/Zip _____

Telephone _____

Email_____

☐ **Please charge my credit card for $10.90.**
(MasterCard, Visa, American Express and Discover cards accepted)

Number _____Exp. Date _____

Signature _____